Mental Toughness

Build an Extreme and Unbeatable Mind. Emotional Intelligence, Willpower, Self Discipline, Self Esteem and Resilience With Leadership's Mindset.

Meditation and Yoga Practice.

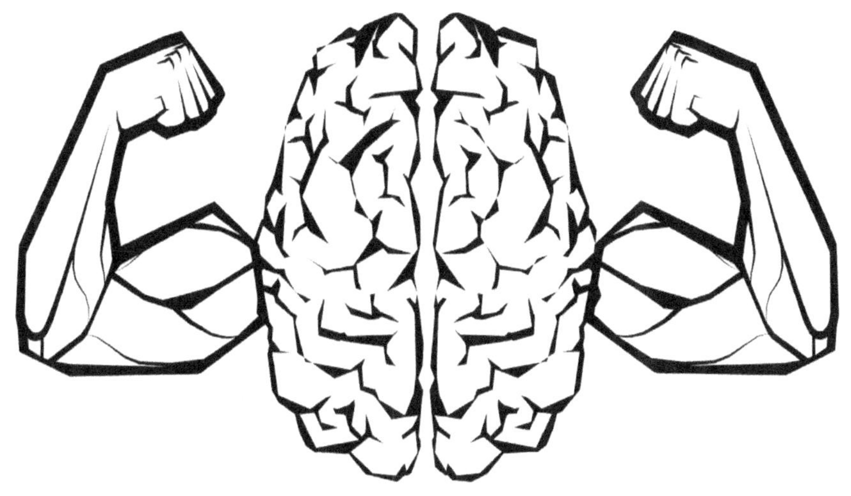

Table of Contents

original author of this work can be in any fashion deemed liable for any hardship or damages that may befall them after undertaking information described herein.

Additionally, the information in the following pages is intended only for informational purposes and should thus be thought of as universal. As befitting its nature, it is presented without assurance regarding its prolonged validity or interim quality. Trademarks that are mentioned are done without written consent and can in no way be considered an endorsement from the trademark holder.

Introduction

Developing and maintaining mental toughness can help you understand and do what must be done in times of hardship. Mental toughness is all about being able to overcome past failures by staying competitive and positive. You have to train and prepare yourself to be mentally prepared for the challenges that may come your way. Mental toughness will give you the strength you need to cope with your inadequate performance or mistakes. It also gives you the resilience needed to keep going regardless of these adversities. You can't lose your resolve or focus even when things don't go as planned. By being mentally tough, you continue to persevere through the hardships you face.

Mental toughness can be developed by practicing self-talk, establishing routines, and using visualization techniques. Self-talk strategies can boost mental toughness and confidence in different settings, such as school and work. Personal pep talks, creating a list of achievements and developing personal affirmations can encourage fortitude and perseverance and improve mental toughness when your self-confidence plummets. Self-talk is more effective when it's realistic. For instance, you are going to compete in a billiards tournament. You can say that you're going to win against your opponent because you've been playing for years.

The ability to maintain control over the mental aspect of your performance can boost your confidence and give you a calmer and clearer state of mind. These benefits may help you get the positive outcome you're looking for. Developing mental toughness requires practice. It's not easy, but you only need to practice, and success will follow.

Routines allow you to trust the process. When you have a comprehensive performance routine, you don't have to think. Thinking is among the most dangerous activities an athlete or performer can do. While thinking is a crucial part of creating a strategy before a play, it prevents you from trusting your highly practiced skills inherent talent and from being in the moment. A well-developed routine can help athletes and performers do what their coaches tell them from the sidelines. They can focus on a series of actions or words that they need to do.

Visualization is also essential in maintaining mental toughness. You should visualize positive results and stay realistic at the same time. Expect the unexpected. Your visualization should be thorough and include precisely what you want to get. You should also think about changes in plans and any errors that might occur. It's important to stay calm and confident, even if things are not going as planned. Always hope for the best.

Staying confident may seem easy, but when the stakes and pressure are high, it's more complicated than it seems. It is easy to get discouraged, mainly if you didn't do well. Developing mental toughness can help you deal with challenges that may come your way. Read this ebook and learn everything you need to know about mental toughness.

Chapter 1: What is Mental Toughness?

Mental toughness determines a person's ability to show a consistent performance under pressure and stress. This personality trait is closely associated with perseverance, character, grit, and resilience. You have to be aware of your emotions and thoughts. Mindfulness is all about working with your emotions and thoughts to consciously decide your actions. In other words, it is all about responding instead of reacting.

Mental strength is not about acting tough. You don't need to ignore your emotions to say that you're mentally tough. The image that comes to mind when someone says a mentally strong person is a cold, domineering, unemotional, and aggressive individual who never seeks help. This is wrong. Mental strength is about realizing how your emotions affect your behaviors and thoughts. It is not about ignoring emotional or physical pain. It is about knowing the source of pain and when to listen and when to oppose.

You don't need to be self-reliant to show that you are mentally tough. Mental toughness is about realizing and acknowledging that you don't have all the skills and answers. You are willing to grow and seek help from other people. Mental toughness is not just about positive thinking. You have to think logically and sensibly. Excessive optimism can be as bad as pessimism.

Mental toughness is not only about achieving happiness. You don't have force yourself to feel happy. Mental toughness is about achieving your full potential. You can still be mentally tough if you have anxiety, depression, or other issues. Although developing mental toughness needs more work, the result will be worth it.

Origins

Mental toughness has origins in sport and academic research. Its origins in sport are wider and stronger than in academic research. Norman Triplett, a psychologist, performed the first documented sport psychology experiment in 1898. He found out that cyclists who are competing with others in a race were faster than those in individual time-trials. Social influence motivated them.

In 1925, Coleman Griffith conducted a study on the effects of psychological characteristics on a person's sports performance. Griffith is considered as the sport psychology founder. In the late 1960s, sports psychologists began working together. Coaches and players in professional sports soon started to take notice of the effects of psychological characteristics on one's performance. Vince Lombardi, an NFL coach, enjoyed great success due to working with athletes to eliminate doubt and convincing them that victory was the only satisfactory result. Lombardi is sometimes called the father of mental toughness.

The USOC or U.S. Olympic Committee started expressing interest in sport psychology's potential in the 1980s. A registry of qualified sport psychologists was established in 1983 to give referrals to athletes who wished to boost the mental aspect of their performance.

Dr. Jim Loehr realized that the same ideology could be used in business. He published books that emphasize the significance of applying focus and energy to be completely engaged in the task at hand. Mental toughness assessments can be used to choose who can be placed in high-stress positions and still succeed.

Just like athletes, business leaders have to improve their game. Here are the characteristics of mental toughness that leaders have to develop.

- ❖ **Resiliency** – You need to learn how to stay positive and recover fast when faced with adversity.
- ❖ **Sportsmanship** – Handle personal attacks with composure.
- ❖ **Responsiveness** – Responsiveness pertains to how fast you can adapt and how you can successfully make decisions under pressure.
- ❖ **Determination** – You may come across various odds, but you should stay confident and strong. Your perseverance will help you get your desired results.

- ❖ **Moral Values and Courage**– Acting with courage and confidence makes it easy to easier to follow the rules and make the right decisions.
- ❖ **Flexibility** – You must stay flexible and look for a way to go forward. You should be able to adapt to changes instead of being defensive about a method that is not working.

Mental Toughness Coaching

Employees should be provided with tools for success. Mental toughness coaching is beneficial in industries where there's heavy competition. High-stress occupations such as military personnel, emergency responders, and medical workers can also benefit from mental toughness coaching. Any job can be taxing for a person who is not mentally tough.

Mental toughness coaching can be used to manage stress. It can be beneficial for children as well. A resilient person can face life's challenges and deal with the pressures they will face. Mental toughness training can also be included in other demanding pursuits. Professionals who need to compete in aggressive environments can benefit from this.

Can You Measure Mental Toughness?

Yes! If you are looking for a way to achieve your athletic goals faster, you can start by measuring your mental toughness. Mental toughness is vital to success, but you don't know how to build and maintain it. In making things simpler, mental toughness is about focusing on your goals and not being distracted by anything. You can make a game plan to build measurable mental toughness.

First, let's talk about increasing your focus on a particular goal. Before any competition or practice, you should ask yourself what you want. If you are going to do your best, your goal should be worthwhile. It must be something you have not achieved yet. Your goal should excite and inspire each time you think of it. It's also essential that you know what steps you should take to achieve your goals. Don't try to improve multiple skills at the same time. By choosing and improving only one skill, you can focus and master it. After mastering that skill, you can move on to another one.

You should also ask yourself if you're ready to succeed. By answering this question consciously and positively, you're setting the belief that you'll succeed. Since you have a goal and you know the steps that should be done to achieve it, you have to tell your body that success is your only choice.

It's also important to limit distractions. One of the best ways to reduce distractions is to create a short, constructive phrase. A simple phrase is easier to remember. It will also be easier and faster to form a habit. Repeat your goals to yourself if you encounter distractions. This way, you will be able to focus on the path to success.

You have to be prepared for the unexpected as well. The surprise is among the reasons people lose focus. By expecting and embracing distractions, you can forget about it and focus on the skills that will help you accomplish your goals and succeed. If you make mistakes, you shouldn't beat yourself up over it. Don't try to seek perfection. Instead, seek improvement.

Tools for Measuring Mental Toughness

If you want to attain your goals faster, you should actively measure mental toughness. Different tools have been developed for such purposes such as the AFMTI (American Football Mental Toughness Inventory) and the SMTQ (Sports Mental Toughness Questionnaire). MTQ48is another tool used to measure mental toughness.

According to Dr. Lee Crust, both MTQ48 and SMTQ seem to tap MT's core components. However, MTQ48 offers a more comprehensive measure of mental toughness. Doug Strycharczy and Peter Clough developed this tool. It measures the 4 components of MT identified by Strycharczy and Clough. These components are confidence, control, challenge, and commitment.

Confidence pertains to a person's self-belief in his abilities. It also refers to the interpersonal confidence you have to deal with challenges and to influence other people. Mentally tough individuals have the inner strength to stand up for themselves and are confident to handle the situation. Their confidence allows them to stand for their views bravely and be comfortable in dealing with objections

Control is about your sense of self-worth. It also pertains to the extent to which you feel in control of your life and how you control the display of your emotions. A mentally tough person will deal with it regardless of how they feel. Their positive outlook can often boost the mental state of those around them.

Challenge pertains to the extent to which you will push back your limits, accept the risk, and embrace change. It is also about how you see both the good and bad outcomes. A mentally tough person sees adversity, challenges, and adversity as opportunities instead of threats. They will grab the chance to thrive in an unknown situation. A mentally tough person with a high challenge score will usually enjoy new people, places, creativity, and innovation.

Commitment pertains to how ready you are to set goals for what you have to do. It's also about your ability to make quantifiable promises that you will work hard to complete. These components affect your mental toughness. You can use MTQ48 to measure and boost your mental toughness.

Stages of Mental Toughness

Mental toughness has 3 primary stages that determine a person's response to stressful situations. The first stage is your ability to identify the stressor and trigger your response to this situation using concentration and concentration.

The second stage is your skill to transform this reaction into performance versus allowing it to be a disability. The third stage is your ability to execute the right leadership strategies and decision making once you learn to direct and control the stress response to the situation.

Signs of a Mentally Weak Person

Some people don't let anything stop them from achieving their goals. Others continuously complain and make up excuses. These people can get controlled easily by others. That is the difference between a mentally strong person and mentally weak individual. Here are the most common signs that a person is mentally weak.

- ❖ **Giving up without a fight**

A mentally weak person will give up easily. Weak people don't persevere. They forget that success won't come to those who quit easily. No matter how difficult the situation is right now, you should fight for your goals. If you quit before you even start, it could mean that you're mentally weak. This could negatively affect your life sooner or later. Problems will come your way at some point, but you shouldn't give up. Quitting, without trying hard means you're mentally weak to overcome problems.

❖ Not stepping out of one's comfort zone

It's easy to set limits and never go past it because it might feel uncomfortable. When you have a small comfort zone, and you refuse to come out of it, you might be mentally weak. It means that when you want big things, you have to leave your comfort zone in order to get it. However, they never get what they want because they're afraid to step out of their comfort zone. Always taking on what you're already familiar with, and never taking risks can amplify your weakness. You won't be able to learn something new if you stay in your comfort zone. Although trying new things can be uncomfortable, it's the only way to defeat weakness.

❖ Complaining a lot

Life has ups and downs. We go through various events and tests that shape our mindset and personality, but we try to rise above the depressing events that occur in our lives. A mentally strong person would remain positive and realize that an unfavorable occasion is not the end of everything. A mentally weak person, on the other hand, tends to whine and complain a lot. They spread negativity, which is troublesome for most people. No one wants to be around a negative person.

A mentally and emotionally strong person will look for ways to solve his problems. You will seldom hear them whine or complain about the negative things that occur to them. They are liable for their actions and always try to see the positive side of things. A mentally and emotionally strong person is willing to deal with problems consciously. They don't have time to feel sorry for themselves.

❖ **No consideration for other people's views or opinions**

You shouldn't allow others to influence your choices, but you should listen to other people's opinions to a certain extent. Mentally and emotionally strong people often have a high ego and seldom listen to anyone but themselves.

❖ **Envying others for their success**

When you always feel envy towards others, you may be actually disappointed in yourself. Your brain can't understand their success in a positive light. Envy interferes with your rational thinking and will harm you in the long run. You should change this habit as soon as possible if you wish to become a strong person.

❖ **Getting angry too easily and quickly**

Some people tend to get angry fast, and others are innately calm. If you get angry too easily and quickly when someone challenges you, you may be actually mentally weaker than others. How you handle the challenges that come your way depends on you. If you allow negative thoughts and frustrations to control you, nothing good will come out of it. You will only push people away and miss opportunities that could improve your life.

❖ **The tendency to be excessively dramatic**

Mentally weak people tend to be extremely dramatic. They try to prove to other people that they have the most challenging and unlucky lives. They don't understand that the brain is programmed in such a way that it projects a person's emotions and thoughts into their life. Mentally and emotionally strong people are able to filter negativity and avoid spreading it onto others one way or another.

These are some of the most common signs of a mentally weak person. If you exhibit some of these signs, you don't need to worry because you can correct it. It all depends on your mindset. If you want to change the current you, feel free to do so. Everything is up to you to decide.

Chapter 2: The Traits of an Unbeatable Mind

You won't be able to achieve your goals if you don't have a daily check-in plan that has no assessment or follow-up of your progress. You have to measure your progress in order to keep your momentum going and ensure that you're in the right direction. Developing an unbeatable mind is also important. These are the traits of an unbeatable mind.

- Exceptional resolve
- Positive attitude
- Discernment
- Calm
- Single point focus
- Humble acceptance
- High tolerance to pain

Unbeatable Mind Training

You have to condition your mind to be unmatched. The first step is to gain control of the mind and charge it with positive energy. You have to build an unbeatable vision in your mind and nurture this vision through constant internal visualization practice. The last step is taking massive action.

Sitting silently and observing thoughts will help you avoid distractions and empower your witness. Meditation practices like Vipassana and Zen use this technique as well. As your awareness of witness improves, you will be in full control when negative thought patterns emerge in your conscious mind. If you don't eliminate these negative thought patterns, they will grow until they temporarily control your behavior and mind.

One of the best ways to stop these negative thought patterns is to have a power statement. The words "stop" and "no" are also negative, so you're just boosting the negative energy. It is better to use positive statements such as "I am completely in control." In other words, you need to find a powerful, meaningful, and positive statement to you. Practice this statement until it becomes second nature to use when negative thoughts pop up in your mind.

You also need to have a "what's next" strategy because if you don't have one, your mind might just return to the same unconstructive pattern. Think of a positive thought pattern that motivates you and supports your goals. Maintain this new thought pattern with a meaningful positive statement that you can repeat to yourself. For instance, you can say that you are "feeling and looking good." You can follow this statement with "ought to be a model."

Remember that your breath and your thoughts are the only things that can be controlled in life. Any negative thought pattern is first seen, stopped and replaced with a positive pattern. It is maintained with an affirmative mantra.

Disciplines of an Unbeatable Mind

- **Self-mastery**

Self-mastery is all about training and practicing the core components of development crucial to living a good life. These components include the heart, subconscious development, and mental toughness, physical readiness, intuition, and awareness as well as emotional control and depth. Self-mastery also promotes devotion, simplicity, introspection, contentment, authenticity, and sincerity.

- **Service**

Service should be selfless and promote generosity, empathy, and abundance. Self-mastery and service should be developed together.

The most critical part when training your mind is identifying and diffusing threats. Developing and maintaining an unbeatable mind is a lifelong process. If you don't push yourself to try new things or continuously challenge yourself, you will get mushy. Setting challenging goals yearly and working to achieve them will help you develop an unbeatable mind.

Chapter 3: Resilience

A resilient person knows how to deal with hardship and stress. Resilience is the mental pool of strength that you can summon in times of need to overcome hardships without falling apart. A resilience person can handle adversity better than someone who is not. Everyone experiences setbacks at some point in their life. How you deal with the challenges that come your way plays an essential role in the outcome and long-term psychological consequences you will experience. Some of these adversities might be minor such as not getting the dress you want to buy, while others are devastating, such as typhoons and hurricanes.

What is Resilience?

Resilience pertains to a person's ability to handle setbacks and problems. A resilient person can use his strengths and skills to recover from problems such as natural disasters, job loss, divorce, financial problems, medical emergencies, and illness. They don't hide from problems or fall into despair. A resilient person faces challenges head-on. This doesn't mean that they feel less anxious or feel less distress and stress than other people. It only means that a resilient person is capable of handling difficulties in a manner that promotes growth and strength. The problems they are facing may boost their mental strength and resiliency even further.

Those who lack resilience may become overwhelmed by the challenges and setbacks they are facing. They may use harmful coping mechanisms and wallow in despair. Failure or disappointment might cause them to adopt dangerous or destructive behaviors. Those who lack resilience slowly recover from challenges and may suffer from more psychological distress than others.

Resilient people understand that problems happen and that life has ups and downs. Resilience doesn't rid of stress or difficulties in life. Resilient people still experience the grief, sense of loss, and pain that comes after a misfortune. However, their mental outlook lets them overcome such emotions and recover. Resilience gives them the strength to deal with setbacks head-on, move on, and overcome adversity.

Resilience vs. Mental Toughness

Mental toughness and resilience are not the same. These terms are frequently used interchangeably. All mentally tough people are resilient. However, not all resilient people are mentally tough. The main difference between mental toughness and resilience lies in a positive aspect. Experiential learning helps a person develop mental toughness. This can be done through simply living through life experiences, targeted development, or coaching.

The result might be different, but crucial in an environment where we experience challenges, setbacks, and changes faster and more frequently than before. It's important to have a positive mindset. By doing so, you can accept setbacks as a natural part of life. Mental toughness helps you succeed, and resilience helps you survive. You get a positive result, and this leads to better well-being and performance and development of positive behaviors.

Some people naturally remain composed even when faced with challenges, but these behaviors are not only innate traits found in a few individuals. Many experts say that resilience is common. People can learn the skills needed to become more resilient. Social support contributes to resilience. Mentally strong individuals tend to have their loved ones' support. Their support systems encourage them during times of trouble.

Other factors that contribute to resilience include the ability to create realistic plans and follow them, having optimistic opinions of themselves and their skills, being an excellent communicator, and managing emotions efficiently.

Traits of Resilient People

People have different coping skills, but researchers have identified some common characteristics of resilience. The good news is that many of these traits can be developed and improved to help you deal with life's challenges. Resilient individuals know their situations, the behavior of people around them, and their own emotions. You have to understand what's causing your feelings and why in order to manage them effectively.

Resilient individuals can maintain control over their situation and think of ways to deal with problems. They also understand that life has many challenges. We can't avoid these problems, but we can stay flexible, open, and ready to adapt to changes. Here are the characteristics of resilient people.

- **Excellent problem-solving skills**

Resilient people can identify the solution to their problem that will lead to their desired result. Sometimes, people develop tunnel vision when they're in a dangerous situation. They fail to leverage opportunities or notice essential details. Resilient people are capable of rationally and calmly looking at problems and thinking of a successful solution.

- **Viewing themselves as a survivor**

Resilient people see themselves as a survivor when dealing with problems. Don't see yourself as a victim. What you should do is look for ways to solve the problem. Stay focused on positive results.

- **Sense of Control**

Resilient people tend to possess an internal locus of control. These individuals believe that their actions will affect the result of an event. Some factors are outside of your personal control like natural calamities. However, you should think that you have the authority to make choices that will influence your situation, future, and skill to cope.

- **Support systems**

When you're dealing with problems, having a support system can make things easier for you. Talking about the problems you are facing can be an excellent way to express your emotions, gain new perspectives and look for solutions. Online support groups, friends, colleagues, and family members can be your support system.

When to Seek Help

You've identified yourself as a resilient person. Being resourceful is a good trait, but you should also know when to seek help. When facing problems, you can seek help from counselors and psychologists who are trained to handle emergencies. Here are some of the best sources of support.

- **Support Groups**

Support groups are composed of people who can give support and compassion to those who need help. It's a great place to talk about the problems and challenges you are facing.

- **Books**

You can read books about people who have overcome similar problems. This can motivate you as well as give you ideas on how to deal with the issue you are facing right now.

- **Psychotherapy**

See a mental health professional if you can't deal with the problem on your own. This professional will help you face the problem, determine your strengths, and build new coping skills.

- **Online Communities**

Online message boards can be a good place to talk about various issues with people who have faced the same problems. They can offer continual support and motivate you.

How to Improve Resilience

Whether you want to improve your coping skills or you are going through a difficult time right now, improving your resilience is essential. Here are some tips on how to improve your resilience.

- **Be optimistic**

It's challenging to stay optimistic when you are facing a problem, but you should maintain a positive outlook. Having a positive mindset doesn't mean that you should ignore the issue to focus on a positive result. A resilient person understands that problems are temporary, and he has the skills to fight these challenges. You may be in a difficult situation right now, but you should stay positive and hope for a bright future.

- **Know your purpose in life**

Knowing your purpose in life can help you recover from whatever adversity you are facing right now. Cultivate your spirituality and become more involved in the community. Participate in meaningful activities.

- **Accept change**

A resilient person is adaptable. By embracing change and learning how to be flexible, you will be able to respond better to a life crisis. You can use this chance to take a new direction. Some people can't adapt to sudden changes. A highly resilient person, on the other hand, can adapt to changes and succeed.

- **Having confidence in your abilities**

A resilient person believes in his ability to cope with life's challenges. According to research, self-esteem plays a crucial role in recovering from tough events and dealing with stress.

You should remind yourself of your achievements and strengths. When negative thoughts pop up in your mind, replace them immediately with positive ones like you're good at your job and you can do what you want to do. Be more confident in your ability to cope with a crisis because this is a good way to build resilience and mental toughness.

- **Social support**

Social support is essential for a person's health and overall well-being. Having supportive people around you is particularly beneficial when you are in a tough situation. Talking about your situation with a family member or friend will not make your problem go away, but it lets you get positive feedback, shares your emotions, determine possible solutions to the problem and get support.

- **Set goals**

Resilient people can realistically see crisis situations and set sensible goals to solve the problem. When you find overwhelmed, you need to take a break to assess what you are facing. Think of possible solutions and split them into manageable steps.

- **Take care of yourself**

It is easy to neglect your needs when you are stressed. A person who doesn't adapt well to a crisis situation often loses appetite, refuses to exercise, and lacks sleep. You should focus on improving your self-nurturance ability even when you are facing a problem. This includes making time for activities that you love. Doing so will help you boost your resilience and overall health. Moreover, you will be prepared to face any challenge that may come your way.

- **Develop problem-solving skills**

According to research, those who can think of solutions to problems can cope with setbacks a lot better than those who can't. When you face a new challenge, create a list of the possible ways to solve the problem. Try various methods and develop a reasonable way to solve common problems. If you practice your problem-solving skills regularly, you will be ready to face serious challenges.

- **Solve problems by taking action**

Don't wait for the problem to disappear. If you do, you will just prolong the crisis. You should work on solving the problem immediately. There may not be a simple or quick solution, but you can always take steps to make your current situation less stressful. You should focus on your progress and plan your next steps. Don't be disheartened by the amount of work that you still need to do. Actively thinking of solutions will help you feel in control of your life. Instead of only waiting for something to happen, you should be proactive in order to achieve your goals.

Resilience takes time to develop and maintain. Don't get disheartened if you are still struggling to handle problematic situations. You can learn to be resilient, and you don't need to develop a specific set of actions to be one. Resilience can differ significantly from one person to another. You can practice the common traits of resilient people and improve your current strengths as well.

Chapter 4: Why Develop Mental Strength

Mental strength is essential for everyone because it explains the behavior of the person you're dealing with. It also improves your productivity and efficiency. Mental strength makes you more careful about the work you're doing. Good mental strength actually has a direct effect on a person's educational achievements. Mental strength makes up for almost 25 percent of the disparity of one's performance during exams. According to studies, the same thing can be observed in large organizations and groups of people. Mental strength doesn't only improve your performance. Here are the other benefits of mental strength.

✓ **Greater goals**

There's a link between personal aspirations and mental strength. Those who are mentally strong tend to be more determined than mentally weak people. They want to be better, and they know they're capable of getting what they want as long as they put in the required effort.

✓ **Show positive behaviors**

Mentally strong people tend to show positive behavioral patterns. They have a positive outlook and positive traits.

These people don't walk away from problems. Instead, they face these issues and deal with them head-on in a positive way.

✓ Find and keep a job

There's also a link between a person's ability to find and keep a job and mental strength. In institutions that provide higher education, students with good mental strength tend to complete their studies and get good grades than mentally weak people. The latter is more likely to quit along the way.

✓ Achieve a better sense of well-being

Mentally strong people tend to have a better sense of wellbeing than mentally weak individuals. They are more capable of handling adversities and bad days. Mentally strong people are also less likely to be absent in school or work. They're less likely to get involved in bullying. People with high mental strength can recover from setbacks faster because they know to consider things in various perspectives. They also tend to have a better sleep at night, which helps them function better the next day.

Mental strength can be developed. Almost anyone can develop mental strength. This will be a valuable asset throughout your life.

Chapter 5: How to Build Mental Strength

Developing mental toughness usually happens by teaching a person how to deal with stress much more effectively. This is done by making basic changes to how you think about setbacks and challenges. You are also taught with the strategies and techniques that mentally strong people use to deal with adversaries. What worked for others may not work for you, so the approach for each person may be different. Here are some tips on how to build mental strength.

- **Forget about the things you cannot control**

Don't waste your resources on things you cannot control. It could be global warming or politics. However, it doesn't matter what things you have control over because you want other people to care. You can do whatever you want to do. Decrease your carbon footprint or vote for the person you find trustworthy. You can try to change yourself, but you don't try to make others change. They will not yield to your request, so why waste time on something you won't benefit from.

- **Act as if you're in control all the time**

Many people believe that luck plays an integral part in one's failure or success. If they're successful at what they are doing, they will say that luck favored them. If they fail, they will say that luck was against them. Most successful people feel that good luck contributed to their success, but they don't worry about bad luck or wait for good luck. They act as if success or failure is totally within their control. If they succeed, they caused it. If they fail, they also caused it. They don't waste mental energy, thinking about what happened to you. This way, they can do their best to make things happen.

- **Celebrate other people's success.**

Resentment is never a good trait. It sucks up a large amount of mental energy that is better used elsewhere. When a loved one does something great, that doesn't mean you can't do the same thing. The success of other people should inspire you to do your best as well. Embrace and create awesomeness, and you will definitely benefit a lot from doing so.

- **Don't allow yourself to criticize, whine or complain**

Words have power over you, so whining or complaining about your problems will only make you feel worse. If something doesn't go as planned, don't complain because it is just a waste of time. Put your mental energy into thinking of solutions that will make the situation better. Don't think about what is wrong. Instead, think about how to make things better. Do the same for your colleagues or friends. Don't allow them to whine. Instead, give them valuable advice to make their lives better.

- **Learn from mistakes and let it go**

When you commit a mistake, you should see it as a chance to learn something new. Your mistakes don't define you. Think of how you're going to make sure that next time, you will know how to ensure everything goes right. If a loved one or another person makes mistakes, you should also see it as a chance to be understanding, kind, and forbearing.

- **Be thankful for your blessings**

Don't worry about what you don't have. Instead, think of what you have right now. Be grateful for your blessings, and you will feel better. It's the best way to recharge your mental battery.

- **Impress yourself**

You can't please everyone and while people may like your clothes, title or possessions, that doesn't mean that they really like you. What you want to have is a genuine relationship with the people around you. This can only be achieved when you start trying to be yourself and stop trying to please others. You will have the more mental energy for those who really care about you.

What Impressing Yourself Means

Today, we can easily show our adventures, accomplishments, and purchases through social media. Instead of thinking about personal success, we try to impress people with these accomplishments every day. We have lost the desire to impress ourselves. However, you should actually work on impressing yourself. You are your biggest critic. If you can't affirm yourself, it's possible that you are not great at affirming other people. Everyone deserves to be happy. You can start by allowing yourself to be impressed by the things you do without fear of discrimination or judgment from other people.

This is how you start impressing yourself. It doesn't matter how little your progress is. Your achievement maybe cooking a new dish or buying a new dress. You should inspire and motivate yourself every day to be consistently impressive. Your home plays an essential role in your journey to improve and impress yourself.

You have to feel good about the space you have made. If you don't love your place, you should create a new environment. It is not just about what you placed in your home. It's about what you do with your home. Remember that your home environment creates lasting memories, and you want these memories to be happy. You can start by finding furniture that suits you. For instance, look for a bed that you will allow you to sleep tightly at night. You want to feel at home in your own home, so don't settle for less.

Tips to Impress Yourself

We want to impress others, and it's completely natural. We want them to know our capabilities and be liked. However, we forget to be ourselves in exchange for this desire to please others. You only need to impress yourself. What is most important is how you really feel about yourself. You're special, and you should know that. Follow these tips to impress yourself.

❖ **There's no need to inform others that you are not ditzy**

When someone says mean things about you, don't mind them. Who cares about what they think? They don't know who you really are. Just know how you really feel about yourself. When someone tells you that you're ditzy, does it mean that you really? No! Assess yourself and your actions.

❖ **You don't need others to reassure you that you're smart**

It may be nice to hear others say that you are smart, but what is most important is that you believe you're smart. If others are testing your knowledge, tell them that you're not up to it. You don't have to prove your intelligence to anyone.

❖ **Don't wear makeup just to impress others**

Wearing makeup makes you feel great. That's enough reason to wear makeup. You don't need to wear it just to impress others.

❖ **You don't have to tell others that you're exercising**

What's most important is that you want to get fit and you're doing it for yourself. If you love swimming, you can take swimming lessons. Do the things you love and take as many photos of what you're doing if it makes you happy. You are exercising to get your desired body, not to impress other people.

❖ **You don't have to label yourself to impress others**

You know how you feel about yourself, so you don't have to be labeled as attractive or smart just to feel good. There's no need for other people to tell that you're handsome or beautiful. It feels great to know that people think you're good-looking. However, you already know that you're beautiful in your way. Perhaps you're attractive by your acumen, or you have beautiful hair. Assess your own beauty and if someone says that you're attractive, thank them because it's a compliment.

Always remember that you only need to impress yourself. You don't have to impress anyone. Evaluate yourself and amaze yourself by your actions. Look for your best qualities that make you stand out. Appreciate your gifts, and you will gain more self-esteem from that.

Chapter 6: Fear and Stress

Fear is our natural emotional reaction to perceived dangers and threats. It can be crippling and uncomfortable, but don't let fear control you. Feeling fear is not a sign of weakness or abnormal. It's an emotion just like happiness and sadness. The ability to be afraid is normal. If you don't feel fear, it's a sign that there's something wrong with your brain. Fear allows us to assess our environment and possible threats to our wellbeing. It also allows us to make decisions based on possible outcomes and past events.

There are times when fear overwhelms us. The more you listen to the possibility of dangers and think about fear, the more overwhelming it appears to become. When this happens, it can affect every aspect of your life, scramble your logical thought process, and erode your confidence. Always remember that fear is only an emotion. The mind evaluates an event and assigns a level of significance and emotion. The brain stores it in a manner that when that event or something similar happens again, an action can be done much more efficiently and faster. Here are other things you need to know about fear.

- **Things will seem scarier when you're already afraid**

Potentiation is a process wherein your fear response is augmented if you're already afraid. For instance, the slightest turbulence will make you feel nervous if you're afraid of flying. You also need to know that fear isn't as instinctive as you believe. Some fears are automatic, while others are learned. For instance, pain causes fear automatically as it affects your survival.

A good example of a learned fear is when you learn to be afraid of a specific situation, person, or place due to negative past experiences or associations. For example, you may be afraid to get close to the sea if you had a near-drowning experience in the past. Some fears are taught. For instance, certain social groups are ill-treated and feared due to an impression created by the society that they are dangerous.

- **There are different kinds of fear**

Fear can be mild to overwhelming. For example, hearing news of a terrorist attack might be paralyzing. Constant worry, daily insecurity, and chronic stress can seriously harm your mental and physical health over time.

- **Fear dictates your actions**

Fight, fright, freeze, and flight are actions dictated by fear. The freeze means stopping what you're doing and focusing on the stimulus to choose what you should do next. The next step is choosing either flight or fight. You decide whether to work around the threat or deal with it directly. You experience fright when you feel overwhelming fear. There's no action taken. You don't flee or flight. Being in fright mode all the time can result in depression and hopelessness.

- **Your actions become more heroic when the threat is real**

We have different reactions to imagined and real threats. Fearing the bad things that may not or may occur in the future makes you anxious. However, you take little action to deal with it. Imagined dangers cause paralysis. You're overwhelmed, but you don't know what to do. Real threats cause frenzy. You take action immediately and without backing down when the threat is about to happen and identifiable. For instance, a serious health scare can motivate you to change your eating habits.

- **You can feel fear even if you're not in danger**

The brain is very efficient that we start to fear different kinds of stimuli that are not present or scary. You feel fear even if there's nothing to be afraid of because of what you imagine could occur. According to neuroscientists, humans are the apprehensive creatures due to our ability to create fears in our mind and to learn and think. However, this objectless fear can result in chronic anxiety and become crippling.

Ways to Fight Fears

Fear can be an ally or an enemy. If you let it control your life, you won't be able to move forward. You will not be able to think clearly when you are flooded with anxiety or fear. Take a break so that you can calm down. You can go for a walk, take a bath, or prepare a cup of tea to distract yourself from your fear or worry for at least 15 minutes.

If your palms are starting to sweat or you're experiencing a faster heartbeat, the best thing to do is to breathe through panic. Feel the fear without trying to divert your attention. Put your palm on your abdomen and breathe deeply and slowly. Your goal is to help your mind become accustomed to coping with panic and eliminate your fear of fear. Here are other ways on how to fight fears.

✓ **Face fears**

Don't avoid your fears because doing so will only make them seem scarier. Your fears should start to fade if you face them. For instance, you're afraid of closed spaces. You can stay a few minutes inside a lift to get rid of your fears.

✓ **Revert to basics**

Many people turn to illegal substances or alcohol to cope with their fears, but doing so will just make things worse. Simple things such as a healthy meal and a good night's sleep can help treat anxiety.

✓ **Don't pressure yourself to be perfect**

Nobody's perfect. It may sound cliché, but it's true. Setbacks and bad days will always occur. However, you don't need to be so hard on yourself. Don't try to be perfect. Life's messy, but you don't need to stress yourself over every little thing.

✓ **Visualize the worst**

Try to imagine the worst thing that can occur. Maybe it is being diagnosed with diabetes or having a heart attack. Try to imagine yourself being diagnosed with diabetes. It is not possible. Your fear will disappear the more you think of it.

✓ **Imagine a happy place**

Close your eyes and think of a calm and safe place. It could be an image of you sleeping on your bed with your spouse next to you or a picture of you eating your favorite dessert. The positive feelings you get from this image will help you stay calm.

✓ **Challenge fearful thoughts**

Challenging fearful thoughts may help you deal with or completely eliminate your fears. If you don't want to take the elevator because you're afraid of getting trapped and suffocating, you should ask yourself if you know someone who has experienced such a thing. Think about what you'd say to someone with a similar fear.

✓ **Talk about your fears**

Talking about your fears makes them seem less scary. Try talking to your family member, partner, or friend. If your fears are not disappearing no matter what you do, you can look for a psychological therapies service to help you.

Don't forget to reward yourself. For instance, you should treat yourself to a meal out or spa when you've made that phone call you've been dreading.

Stress

You know stress when you feel it. The source of stress can be psychosocial, physical, or psychological. You feel threatened by the situation you're facing and doubt your ability to handle it successfully. Severe stress causes fatigue and burnout. We become disillusioned, pessimistic, and cynical. The body is programmed to handle immediate stressful situations by choosing either to fight or to run away.

The adrenal glands produce adrenaline and cortisone. The thyroid gland produces more thyroid hormone to provide the body with more energy to either run or fight. The hypothalamus releases endorphins, which are natural pain killers. Blood is also diverted from your gastrointestinal tract to the muscles, making all of your senses vigilant and alert. These responses can save your life, depending on the threat's nature.

Chronic stress, however, can negatively affect your health. Excessive amounts of cortisone and adrenaline compromise the immune system by reducing your resistance to illnesses, infections, and malignancy. Too much thyroid hormone can cause weight loss and insomnia. It can also make you feel shaky and nervous. Reduction of endorphins can aggravate pain and arthritic aches.

The best way to reduce stress is to create an approach to handle it directly. Avoiding or denying stress only amplifies its impact. How you approach stress depends on the situation. If you have control over the situation, you can actively reduce your stress levels through proper time management. You should also create a game plan for your recreations and careers as well as interact with people you like. If you don't have control over the situation, you can try changing your response to stressful situations. Your attitude is essential, and staying positive is more effective and better than cynical pessimism when it comes to stress.

Another way to deal with stress is to lead a healthy lifestyle. This can be done by nurturing your spirit, accepting your reality, challenging your body, and improving your intellect. You should also follow a healthy diet, get enough sleep, avoid bad habits, and take a break once in a while. Regular exercise, meditation, and improving your social network can also help. Using positive imagery is a good idea, as well. Remember a pleasant past experience or situation. Determine what works for you.

What Stress Feels Like

Stress can produce not only physical symptoms but psychological ones as well. Common physical symptoms of stress include stomachache, headache, muscle tension, shaking, rapid breathing, frequent urination, fast heartbeat, trouble sleeping, sweating, fatigue, dizziness, and diarrhea.

People have different responses to stress. Common psychological symptoms of stress include nervousness or panic, agitation, feelings of imminent doom, unfounded anger, and difficulty concentrating. Experiencing stress for prolonged periods of time can affect your health. People who suffer from chronic stress may develop diabetes, heart disease, panic disorder, high blood pressure, and depression.

Stress comes and goes for most people. It usually happens after a particular life event. Common causes of stress include having an injury or illness, moving, getting married, death of a friend or family member, starting a new job or school and having a baby or a loved one hurt. Regular consumption of illegal substances, alcohol, and caffeine can aggravate the symptoms of stress. Some drugs contain stimulants that make the symptoms worse. These medications include diet pills, thyroid medications, and asthma inhalers.

Stress that seems out of proportion to the trigger or happens frequently may be a sign of an anxiety disorder. Those with anxiety disorders may feel stressed and anxious every day and for long periods of time. One of these anxiety disorders is GAD or generalized anxiety disorder. A common symptom of GAD is uncontrollable worrying. PTSD or post-traumatic stress disorder is caused by a traumatic experience and causes anxiety or flashbacks of that incident.

Another common anxiety disorder is panic disorder. It causes panic attacks or moments of tremendous fear accompanied by shortness of breath, fear of imminent doom, and pounding heart. Obsessive-Compulsive disorder causes recurring thoughts and the urge to complete specific ritual actions. Social phobia causes extreme feelings of unease in circumstances that involve interacting with other people.

It's essential to seek medical help if you are having thoughts about hurting yourself or others. Stress can be treated. There are a lot of strategies and resources that can help. If you can't control your fears and stress is affecting your everyday life, you should talk to your doctor about ways to deal with stress.

Ways to Manage Stress

Know how your mind and body react to stressful situations. When another stressful situation occurs, you will be able to predict your response. Some lifestyle changes can help reduce symptoms of stress. These techniques include identifying what triggers your stress, getting enough sleep, practicing deep breathing, regular exercise, keeping a journal of your feelings, scheduling time for your hobbies, and talking to someone you trust.

If you think you can't deal with stress on your own, your doctor may recommend that you seek a mental health provider. Talk therapy or psychotherapy may be used to help you cope with stress. One of the most effective and popular methods used to manage stress and anxiety is CBT or cognitive behavioral therapy. It teaches the patient to identify anxious behaviors and thoughts and change them into positive ones. Systematic desensitization and exposure therapy may be used to treat the phobia. You will be exposed to anxiety-provoking stimuli gradually to help you deal with your feelings of fear.

Medications may be recommended to treat an anxiety disorder. These medications may include SSRI or selective serotonin reuptake inhibitors like paroxetine and sertraline. Anti-anxiety medications like lorazepam and diazepam may be recommended as well. However, these methods are usually implemented on a short-term basis because of the risk of addiction.

While stress is unpleasant to deal with, it is a condition that can be treated. Some amount of fear and stress should not be cause for concern, but you have to recognize when your fears and stress are negatively affecting your life. Talk to your loved ones about it or seek professional help to get the support you need.

Chapter 7: Goals

A goal pertains to the desired result you envisioned and exerted effort to achieve. It also includes commitment and plans, which will guarantee that your goal is successful. You can't just wait for all daydreaming of owning a business of your own. That's not a goal. You have to take action.

Rules of Goal Achievement

If you want to achieve your goals, you need to have a time-sensitive and detailed action plan. Learn from people who've had similar goals. Surround yourself with individuals who will support you and hold you accountable. You should have confidence in yourself even when nobody else does. Believe that you can accomplish your goals. Your environment may not validate your ideas, but you should still fight for what you want and believe in.

Don't forget to take a break when needed. You shouldn't be too hard on yourself. It's essential to have confidence in everything that you do. Have fun while you're working on accomplishing your goals. This will let you understand your goals more. The journey to accomplishing your goals won't be smooth. There will be obstacles and naysayers along the way, but don't be discouraged. Don't lose sight of your goals. Whether it's a new skill you wish to learn or a country you want to visit, you should be bold and chase your dreams confidently. Believe in yourself, and you can make your dreams a reality.

What are Unreasonable and Reasonable Goals?

Have you shared a goal with your loved ones or friends and found them laughing at what you said? These are what you call unreasonable goals. People usually look down on these ambitions because they are typically considered extremely difficult to achieve, or these people don't understand your goals. What you need to know is that there's no such thing as unreasonable goals.

Goals are defined based on your objectives. You define a goal by understanding the emotions and inner feelings it takes to turn ideas into a reality. All goals and dreams are valid, no matter how strange they might seem. Don't allow public opinion to stop you from chasing your dreams.

Types of Goals

Goals are usually classified as either short-term or long-term. Short-term goals are aspirations that you will accomplish in the near future. This kind of goal is often used as a stepping stone to achieving long-term goals. Short-term goals are viewed as enabling goals as completion of these aspirations will allow you to achieve greater goals. Enabling goals generally, consist of topics such as valuable work experience and education. These factors contribute to your long-term goals. Common short-term goals include getting a summer job, losing 10 pounds of weight, and painting the bedroom.

Long-term goals are composed of plans that you make for your future. Examples of such goals include career, retirement, family, and lifestyle goals. This kind of goal is accomplished over time as you complete the stages of your life. You set long-term goals by visualizing what you want to do and where you wish to be 5 to 25 years from now. Common long-term goals include retiring at 55 years old and building a house. Short-term goals are used to get there.

Short-term and long-term goals can be subdivided. For instance, short-term goals can be classified as either provisional or foundational goals. Long-term goals can be categorized as a capstone or lifetime goals.

- **Provisional Goals**

Provisional goals are usually achieved in less than 1 month. These are generally stepping stones to the bigger goals. Provisional goals are frequently utilized for technical improvements and help you stay focused every day. You may need to accomplish these goals before you work on your foundational goals. For instance, getting a 90 on next week's science test will help you get As on all subjects next semester. This result will help you get into a good school and give you a competitive edge that you can use when applying for a job.

Your provisional goal can also be a separate goal that has no connection to your short-term, lifetime, or capstone goal. The provisional goal you've set could be painting the living room or trimming the grass and shrubs in your garden.

- **Foundational Goals**

Foundational goals are most likely to be completed in less than a year. These are short-term goals can also be individual goals without any connection to lifetime or capstone goals. Examples of such goals include saving money to buy a new TV and learning how to play the violin. Foundational goals may also be enabling goals that must be completed before you work on your capstone goals.

➢ **Lifetime Goals**

Lifetime goals may be completed later on in your life. These are the primary goals that people want to achieve over their lifetime. Lifetime goals are usually completed 10 years in the future. Common examples of lifetime goals include becoming a professional football player, retiring to your dream country and getting a teaching job.

Lifetime goals could be related to career, family, education, pleasure, or financial matters. For instance, you want to become an accountant with a Master's degree, income of $10,000,000, and 4 children. Lifetime goals are usually general at first. They become more defined as you work on your goals. For example, the goal of getting a teaching job can become teaching Trigonometry to high school seniors.

Lifetime goals often are the most significant and meaningful goals. However, these goals are usually achieved later on in your life. As such, you may find it hard to stay focused and maintain a positive outlook toward accomplishing these goals. To prevent this from happening, you should create enabling goals. You write enabling goals to help you accomplish longer-term goals. Enabling goals help you measure your progress.

> **Capstone Goals**

Capstone goals are usually completed within 1 to 10 years. These are generally the key goals that you have to achieve first before you complete your lifetime goals. For example, your lifetime goal is to become a doctor. Your capstone goals should be going to college and then to med school and doing your internship in a hospital.

Reasons Why People Fail to Achieve their Goals

Goals help you focus your resources and efforts as well as avoid distractions. However, not all people can achieve their goals. Here are some of the most common reasons why people fail to get what they want.

➢ Negative mindset

If you have a negative mindset, chances are you won't be able to achieve your goals. You may not even try at all if you expect to fail in the first place. It will be difficult to overcome problems if you're living with fear. Negativity will appear when least expected. If you don't eliminate negativity from the source, it will just return. Negativity will creep into your mind and fill it with discouragement and doubt. It will prevent you from moving forward and grabbing opportunities in the future.

When negative thoughts pop up in your mind, or you catch yourself saying pessimistic words, you should stop and replace them with empowering thoughts and words. Failure to do so will allow your negative words and ideas to overcome your attempt to develop a progressive mindset. Avoid developing a negative mindset by renewing your mind, recalibrating your approach, and refocusing your thoughts. By making these changes, your enthusiasm will become contagious, and you will have more energy to do what you want.

➢ Staying in your comfort zone

The desire to stay in our comfort zone is entirely natural. However, this is also the reasons why we push your dreams and goals to the side. We tell ourselves that we will do it the next day, but nothing really happens. The next day becomes next week and so on.

No action is taken, so don't expect your dreams to become a reality. That "someday" may never come. Don't exhaust your energy and time staying in your comfort zone. Worry, fear, and complacency will keep you locked in this area. Break free and do what you really want to do. Most of the time, you only need to make some slight adjustments in your life to step out of your comfort zone.

> ➤ **Failure to take constant action**

If there's something you want to get, you have to take consistent action. It's a logical and reliable approach that aligns you with your goals daily. This approach is a progressive stance in chasing your goals even when changes are needed. Perhaps you have already spent years researching and modifying the perfect plan but did not take any action.

You've wasted a lot of time doing so. Indeed, you can't regain the time you lost, but you can take action and adapt an approach today to accomplish your goals. You won't be able to achieve your goals overnight, so don't quit and get frustrated when it takes longer than you hoped for.

> ➤ **Being with negative people**

Negative people can destroy your fervor and drain your energy. They will always tell you what can and can't be done. Negative people will constantly notice the negative side of things and tell you about it. Don't surround yourself with negative people. If you listen to them, you will live in the negative. Their negativity will bring down your spirits and discourage you from pursuing your dreams. While you don't have control over what other people say, it's all up to you to decide whether you're going to let them speak in your life. Don't let them affect you. You can prevent them negatively from creeping into your mind and heart.

> **Lacking focus**

If you don't have focus, you won't be able to reach your destination. You may know where you should go, but if you don't have focused directions, it will only be a waste of time. Life's distractions will interrupt you and keep you pushing you back. To get rid of these distractions, you have to refocus your efforts on what's important.

You have to get rid of everything and everyone that won't help you achieve your goals. It's also essential to achieve one goal before working on the next one. If you catch yourself getting off target, you should refocus your mind. Tell yourself what you're aiming to accomplish and your reason for it.

> **Giving in to fear**

Encountering situations that make you feel anxious and uncomfortable is natural. Don't let your fear control you. Determine what you're really afraid of. Fear will hinder your potential and convince you to stay in your comfort zone. It will force you to remain where you are because you think that you will fail if you try something new. Fear comes in various forms and disguises to prevent your success.

If you're aiming for bigger things, fear will convince you that that you're not worthy or capable of achieving them. It will encourage you to quit and avoid trying to accomplish your goals. You should stand up to your fears and tell it to disappear because you have the vision to live and dreams to chase.

> **Trying to accomplish too many goals**

If you try to do too much, you will be overwhelmed at some point. Creating a long list of goals looks impressive, but your passion will fizzle out eventually because it will become impossible for you to achieve all of those goals. You walk away disillusioned and think that setting goals don't work.

Accept the fact that you cannot do everything. You should keep things simpler and targeted. Work on achieving 1 to 2 primary goals at a time. Your goals should be aligned with your vision, purpose, and values. Break down large goals into small manageable steps and begin immediately.

> **Remembering the past**

You can't change what already happened. Don't just relive the past and do nothing at all. Use what you experienced yesterday to improve your current situation. This way, you can lead a better life. You have to do what you need to do right now. If you don't, you will miss today's chances. Don't use your precious time trying to relive what happened in the past. Focus on the present and do your best today.

➢ **Procrastination**

Procrastination causes you to comply or relax without having any intention to accomplish anything. Your actions tell you what's really important to you. Procrastination is all about delaying what you have to do at the moment for tomorrow. That tomorrow, however, never comes for most people. Procrastination prevents you from progressing and leaves you with no excitement or motivation to challenge yourself.

By procrastinating, you're putting your goals, vision, and dreams on hold under the illusion that you'll work on them another day. You make excuses and always delay taking action. It will take unbending commitment and a lot of effort to stop being a procrastinator and become a person who takes action.

➢ **Perfectionism**

Many people want to accomplish certain things, but they ungrateful and insatiable even before they get them. They want to get what they want without putting in a lot of effort. For instance, many people not only to have a high paying job. They also want to be rich right away, which is the wrong approach.

First, you have to be thankful for what you have. It doesn't matter how little or big that is.

When you appreciate what you have, you will feel wealth and realize that you can make it better. You will be motivated to work for what you want to achieve and enjoy the results of your hard work. That is the best way to get rid of perfectionism and still get what you want.

➢ Making excuses

A lot of people make excuses for their situation. They blame everyone and everything for their circumstances. Excuses are roadblocks you've built yourself. These roadblocks prevent you from reaching your true potential and accomplishing what's really possible for you. Your goals will remain a stagnant dream if you keep making excuses. You won't get any results.

When you are committed to achieving your goals, you will not make up excuses. You will be able to do what needs to be done and get your desired results. If you want to reach your full potential, you need to be liable for your life. Learn from the past, take immediate action, and make the necessary changes. You're the only who can accomplish your aspirations.

➢ Failure

Most people are afraid of failure. It is because of this fear that they don't even try in the first place and never see their goals come true. Failure is an opportunity to improve your skills. It shows that you are trying and that you are not quitting. Failure is proof that you are doing everything you can to get what you really want. Experience and lessons follow it. Failure makes you more focused and stronger. It helps you determine what you should and shouldn't do next time. Keep trying, and your efforts will be rewarded eventually.

➢ **Too many expectations**

If you expect too much, you will be disappointed. It is a negative behavior that should be changed immediately. You expect people to act as you want them to and you expect things always to go as planned. When that doesn't happen, you feel dispirited and lose the drive to take action. Get rid of the scenarios playing in your head and accept things as they are. It is also important to remember that there is a path you need to take before you accomplish your goals. This path is composed of many small steps. Big steps make us afraid and anxious. To prevent this from happening, you should break down your goals into smaller steps until you have a list of easy tasks that you can do every day.

Don't just focus on the result. You want to reach your goals faster, and it's normal. However, your impatience is not exactly a good thing. You should enjoy your journey. Focus less on the result, and you will be more motivated to work on your goals.

Chapter 8: Self-confidence, Self Discipline, Willpower and Self-esteem

The terms self-confidence and self-esteem are usually used interchangeably, but they are 2 different concepts. Self-confidence refers to how a person feels about his abilities. Self-esteem, on the other hand, pertains to how a person thinks about himself overall. It develops from situations and experiences that have shaped how you see yourself today. Loving yourself improves your self-esteem, and this increases your self-confidence. When you're confident, your overall self-esteem develops. You can boost your self-confidence and self-esteem at the same time.

What Low Self-esteem Looks Like

When you feel bad about yourself, and you lack confidence, it shows that you have low self-esteem. A person with low self-esteem often feels inept, unlovable, or self-conscious. Other people can easily hurt Their sense of self. They are also hyper-alert and vigilant to signs of rebuff and failure. People who have low self-esteem see disapproval and rebuff even when there is not any. They think that they will make mistakes, do something awkward, or use poor judgment.

Life poses different levels of threats to one's self-esteem. Our self-esteem is weak to others who may openly ridicule or criticize us. However, there's no more significant threat to your self-esteem than you. You are an observer of your feelings, behavior, and thoughts and pass judgment on these phenomena. In other words, you are the most severe critic of yourself. You beat yourself up when you find yourself making a mistake in your judgment, lose self-control, break your promise to yourself, act immaturely, or express yourself awkwardly.

This harsh critic is called the critical inner voice. It is because of this critic that you view yourself negatively. Having a negative perceived self can have grave consequences. For instance, you believe that your colleague doesn't like you. You're more likely to avoid your colleagues, react cynically and defensively or lash out at them.

Your perceived self affects how you interact with others. This perceived self represents an essential foundation for your interpersonal behavior. When you have a negative perceived self, you label yourself as unlovable, self-conscious, or hateful. You find it hard to believe that other people could view you positively.

What Causes Low Self-esteem?

Low self-esteem takes a toll on a person's life. It's difficult to gauge how common poor self-esteem is. However, but several studies have revealed that self-esteem levels drop as people approach their teen years. It's more common for girls to experience this. Low self-esteem can be carried on into adulthood and affect the ability of a person to lead a happy life. What you should keep in mind is that poor self-esteem is not a precise reflection of reality. The cause of poor self-esteem may sometimes be rooted in reality, but it is wrong to assume that you can't change your feelings about yourself

Self-esteem can be changed because it's a state of mind. This will only happen if you are prepared to challenge the negative judgments and feelings you have to yourself. Taking a good look at the darker aspects of your self and your life will help you fight the things that destroy self-esteem. By doing so, your strengths will emerge, and you can put them to good use. Identifying the causes of low self-esteem can be difficult. People suffer from poor self-esteem due to various reasons. However, here are some of the most common causes of low self-esteem. Getting familiar with these causes can help you determine what is destroying your self-esteem. You can do something to improve your sense of worth.

- ***Body Image***

Some people practice unhealthy behaviors to lose weight, such as vomiting, fasting, and skipping meals because they are not happy with their bodies. Body image plays a vital role in a person's self-esteem. We are bombarded with unrealistic images of what the perfect body is. Young women, in particular, are conscious of their body image. The media continually objectifies women's bodies. When their bodies change because of puberty, they don't look like the women they see in music videos or on magazine covers. They may feel inadequate or unattractive because of this.

Young men also suffer from low self-esteem because they don't have the "ideal" body and weight composition. They may feel conscious about their stature as well. Their bodies are seen as a sign of masculinity. As such, young men feel pressured to build large muscles to show their manliness and strength.

- ***Negative Peers***

The way your peers treat, you can significantly affect your self-esteem. If you're part of a social group that doesn't value your feelings and thoughts or respect you and pressures you to do things you are not comfortable with, you might feel that you're unlikeable. You think that the only way for them to like you is to do what they want. This is harmful to your self-esteem. You don't need to cater to anyone. If you don't respect your thoughts and feelings, you can always walk away from them. You don't need negative people in your life.

- ***Negligent or Uninvolved Parents***

A person's feelings are heavily influenced by other people, especially their guardians or parents. However, some people don't get enough support and care at home. Guardians or parents with substance abuse and mental health issues may not be able to provide children with the attention, care, and guidance they need. This is damaging to their self-esteem.

- ***Trauma***

Emotional, physical, sexual, or any form of abuse causes feelings of humiliation and guilt. The victim may feel that they are not worthy of the love, care, and respect of the abuser and that they deserve the abuse. Those who have suffered abuse may develop depression and anxiety associated with the abuse. Their trauma can interfere with their ability to live a happy and fulfilling life.

- ***Existential Crisis***

Young people may find themselves overwhelmed by factors beyond their control. They feel powerless, worthless, and inefficient because of this. Young people and even adults may go through an existential crisis or the time when the meaning of their life is called into question. They can't find answers to questions like what their purpose in life is and why they matter. This inability can hurt their sense of self-worth.

- ***Unrealistic Goals***

Some people expect too much of themselves. The pressure may come from their parents, peer, or themselves. For instance, those who do well academically may expect to the best in everything that they do. People who want to become popular may expect everyone to know and like them. You can't expect everyone to like you and that's a fact of life. If you set unrealistic goals and you don't achieve them, you may feel inadequate and that you're a failure.

- ***Previous Bad Decisions***

You have made bad choices in the past, but you should not dwell in your mistakes. Maybe you have participated in harmful activities in the past, such as drug use. Perhaps you have not been a good child to your parents in the past. Don't think that you're just the type of person who acts in those ways. You may not like yourself due to your past decisions, but you can always change and be a better person. Make decisions that strengthen your negative self-review.

- ***Pessimistic Thoughts***

Talking and thinking about yourself in a certain manner will become a habit. Perhaps you are familiar with the term muscle memory. Once you have performed a specific physical activity many times, your brain will automatically signal the muscles to do what that activity requires. Feelings and thoughts work in the same manner every so often. If you always think negative thoughts or have often felt that you're inferior, you are most likely to think and feel the same way unless you challenge your pessimistic feelings and thoughts about yourself.

These are not the only causes of poor self-esteem, but they are quite common. Assess your situation at home, in your social groups, in school, or at work. You should also review your thoughts and attitude about your goals, body, a sense of purpose, and past decisions to determine any possible cause of low self-esteem. The more you recognize your challenges with self-esteem, the more aware you become of improvements that you can do. Positive changes will then follow.

Tips to Improve Your Self-confidence

Fear of failure is one of the things that stop us from pursuing our dreams. Most people lack the confidence to overcome that fear. How can you beat this fear of failure? The answer is simple. You have to work on your self-esteem and self-confidence. This may not be easy, but it's the best way to get what you want. You might still have fears, but you know that you can overcome them and achieve success. Here are some tips on how to boost your confidence.

- ***Groom Yourself***

A simple shower can do a lot for your self-image and self-confidence. Grooming yourself will not just improve your mood. It's also part of proper hygiene. Dressing nicely will make you look presentable and feel great about yourself. You don't have to wear a $500 outfit. Casual clothes that look presentable are enough.

- ***Speak Slowly***

How you speak can make a significant difference in how other people see you. Someone with authority and in authority speaks slowly. This manner of speaking shows how confident they are. Someone who feels inferior and that he's not worth being heard will speak fast because he doesn't want to keep other people waiting.

Maybe you don't feel confident about speaking slowly. Do it a few times, and your confidence level will improve. You don't need to speak very slowly. Just don't sound too rushed, and you will able to convey your message to your listeners.

- ***Observe Proper Posture***

Remind yourself to stand tall. Proper posture shows your confidence. It is also good for your overall health. If you slouch all the time, you might suffer from back pain and other health problems. Aside from observing proper posture, you should also work on increasing your competence. You can do that by learning something new and practicing.

For instance, you want to become a skilled writer. Don't try to undertake the entire writing profession at once. You should start writing more. For example, you can do some freelance writing or write blogs and short stories. This way, you will be able to improve your writing skills. Allocate at least 30 minutes every day to write.

- ### *Work On Your Self-Image*

Your self-image means a lot to you. The mental image of yourself determines how confident you are in yourself. However, this mental image is not fixed. It can be changed. Improve your self-image by using your mental Photoshop skills. If the mental image you have is not a good one, you should determine why you view yourself that way. Look for a way to fix this image.

- ### *Know Yourself*

Your greatest enemy when you want to replace a negative self-image with self-confidence is yourself. This is why you should find out more about yourself. Listen to your thoughts and write a diary about yourself. You can write about your thoughts and assess why you have such pessimistic thoughts. Think about what you like and what you are good at. Think about what limitations you have and whether they are genuine limitations or only ones you have allowed to take root and bother you.

- ### *Be Kind*

Being generous with yourself and kind to other people is a great way to boost your self-image. You begin to feel great about yourself and think that you're a good person. This way of thinking boosts your self-esteem. You also need to act positively. Just thinking positive is not enough. Action will help you develop self-confidence. When you act on your desire to think positive, you're essentially changing yourself. Don't tell yourself that you can't. Believe in yourself and take immediate action. Your efforts will pay off in the end.

- ***Prepare Yourself***

Being prepared for whatever activity you want to do can boost your confidence. For instance, if you have studied hard for your exam, you will be confident that you will do well. Setting small goals is also better than aiming for larger goals at once. This way, you won't be discouraged. You will feel good about setting smaller goals and achieving all of them. Changing smaller habits will also help. For instance, you can wake up 5 minutes earlier or create a list of your tasks. Practice this for 1 month, and when you have achieved this, you will feel better.

- ***Focus On The Right Solutions***

Don't focus on problems or keep complaining. You should focus on solutions. For instance, you can't motivate yourself. You can't get a 90 on your Math test. How are you going to solve that? If you keep focusing on problems, you won't be able to solve anything.

- ***Smile***

Smile, and you will feel better. Be kind to others. This is a good way to invest your energy and time. It is also better to do something than not do anything at all. Don't be afraid of making mistakes. It is a normal part of life. Use this chance to learn from your mistake, so get active by taking the necessary steps to achieve something. You can try to do some volunteer work. This way, you can spread joy to others and feel better about yourself.

- ***Be More Knowledgeable***

One of the best ways to boost confidence is to empower yourself with valuable knowledge. You can do this by studying and doing more research. The internet is a good place to improve your knowledge. You can also talk to people who've been in a similar situation. Educational institutions, books, and magazines are excellent sources of information as well.

- ***Exercise***

Exercise is an empowering activity, and it can actually make you feel better about yourself. You don't need to go to the gym or buy your own exercise equipment. A 30-minute walk a few times every week would be enough. Exercise is right for your overall health, as well.

Clearing your desk might seem like a trivial thing, but it can work wonders for your concentration. A messy desk can ruin your focus. Clearing off your desk can improve your productivity. You will be able to find what you need easily and quickly.

Boost Your Self-esteem with Proper Grooming

The way you look influences your self-esteem. Looking your best can help you feel better about yourself. Some people may think that driving the most luxurious car, wearing the right dress and having a high paying job is all that's needed to create a good image. However, that's not always the case.

Establishing strong relationships and impressing others takes commitment, dedication, and time. It goes much deeper than just the car that you own or the designer dress you wear. However, it doesn't mean that you should disregard your looks. Our society is image-driven, so most of the first impressions we make are based on appearances. A person's grooming habits are among the first things that people notice. If you keep yourself well-groomed, your self-esteem will increase. You will be more confident to face other people.

You don't have to spend your money and effort trying to imitate the image of models for fitness magazines. However, you should still keep yourself presentable and well-groomed. Your unique image and appearance can speak a lot about your personality. For instance, a man with a clean-shaven face, clean suit and tie, and close-cropped haircut looks like a respectable businessman. A man with a scruffy beard and slightly disheveled long hair will look like a free spirit who doesn't care about what others think of him. Here are some grooming tips that will help you look and feel good.

- ***Wear a pair of high quality shoes***

You might think that your shoes won't be noticed, but our gaze ultimately makes its way down to the floor. In other words, people will always notice what you have on your feet. This is why you should invest in a pair of high quality shoes.

- ***Try different hairstyles***

Trying a different hairstyle or haircut will tell others that you're not afraid to try out something new and be original. Your outer experience influences how other people judge your reliability, skills, sociability, and intelligence. Maintaining the same haircut every year can make you seem boring and unimaginative. There are different hairstyles that you can try, so you can experiment to see which one suits you.

- ***Remove nose hairs***

If you're giving a presentation for a product or trying to impress potential business partners, you don't want those stray nose hairs to distract your viewers. It only takes a minute to trim unsightly nose hairs. Look in the mirror before you go out.

- ***Maintain facial hair***

Many females prefer men who have a beard. If you have started to experiment with different facial hairstyles, you should keep your beard, mustache, stubble or goatee well-taken care of. Invest in a beard comb and beard oil to keep your facial hair under control. If you want to maintain the scruffy and disheveled appearance of a stubble beard, you should buy a high quality trimmer to prevent it from growing too long. If you want to have a goatee, you should keep it well-trimmed. This way, your beard won't make you look sloppy and careless.

- ***Be careful of body odor***

You don't want to lose the respect of your friends or peers because of body odor. If you don't like the smell of aftershave and cologne, you should at least invest in a stick of odorant. If you are a heavy sweater, you should bring your deodorant with you and freshen up in the bathroom.

Other people judge you based on how you portray yourself physically and externally. Proper grooming can help you express outwardly who you are inside. If you pull off these grooming tips, your self-esteem will improve. Other people will also see you differently. Looking well-groomed is crucial for any relationship you want to build and cultivate.

How to Use Your Wardrobe to Improve Your Self-image

Self-image is often associated with how you look and how you dress. You can use your wardrobe to help improve your self-image. Here are some tips on how to do so.

- ***Find a style that suits you***

There are a lot of sources online that give tips on how to pick the right clothes for you. If you're not comfortable in these clothes, you will not feel competent and confident. You should find the styles, fabrics, and clothes that make you feel your best. Which outfit makes you feel attractive and attractive? What are your favorite outfits? After choosing these kinds of styles and clothes, you should get outfits in similar styles. Get rid of the styles and outfits you don't feel great in.

- ***Wear clothes that fit***

If your clothes no longer fit, get rid of them. By holding on to these clothes, you're just tailoring your clothes to the past instead of the present. You should focus on who you are right now and dress in a way that makes you feel good. If you've gained weight, wearing clothes that you're uncomfortable in or are too tight can negatively affect your self-image. You should update your wardrobe instead of beating yourself up because you gained weight. Clothes that don't fit emphasize parts of your body that harm your self-image.

- ***Emphasize your assets***

Showing off your body's assets can boost your confidence. Look in a mirror and determine your best features. It could be your hair, your eyes, or your lips. Once you have identified your best features, you should dress with those assets in mind.

You should choose clothes that compliment and show off your best assets. For instance, your best asset is your legs. You should wear shoes and skirts that emphasize this feature. If your hair is your asset, you should match up colors to compliment this asset. If you want to show off your bust, you should wear V-neck or scoop shirts.

- ***Choose colors that improve your mood***

You should wear clothes that boost your mood. The colors that make you feel great don't need to be bright. You may feel great in white, brown, or black. Pick colors or hues that make you feel good and happy as this can improve your confidence. You can select colors that you feel secure or safe in or complement your skin tone.

- ***Wear clothes that suit your body type***

Dressing for your body type can improve your self-esteem. Choose clothes that complement your figure. People with a pear shape body should emphasize their top half. You can go for slightly flared jeans, A-line skirts, off-the-shoulder tops, and embellished tops.

A person with an apple shape person has a heavier upper body. Wear clothes that draw the eye away from the midsection such as V-necks, shift dresses, long sleeves, flowy tops, high-waist skirts, and straight-leg pants. Don't wear shirts or dresses that bunch at the waist. Choose clothes that show off your legs.

People with a rectangular shape body can add weight or curves to their desired areas by dressing right. Adding belts to outfits is a good choice. You can also go to cinched shirts or dresses. Choose tops with embellishments or ruffles. Wear leggings, skinny jeans, and miniskirts to show your legs.

A person with an hourglass figure has a small waist and curves. Crop tops, pencil skirts, belted jackets, and wrap dresses can emphasize your curves and waist.

Men who have broader shoulders should go for shirts that properly fit them. Those who have a smaller upper body can wear a jacket or layer shirts to add bulk. Men who have more weight around their midsection can go for vertical stripes or darker colors. Avoid horizontal stripes. Those who have a smaller upper body can wear skinny pants. Men whose middle is quite wide can wear straight pants.

- ***Disguise your flaws using your wardrobe***

Having flaws should not affect your self-image. If you want to hide your flaws, you can use your wardrobe to do that. Dressing for your shape is one of the best ways to conceal your flaws. You can also use your clothes to hide the features you hate the most. For instance, you should wear pants that fit you and shirts that are not too tight if you want to hide your belly fat. If you don't like your legs, you should wear leggings or pants that fit you nicely. If you don't like your arms, you should wear tops with sleeves.

- ***Wear jewelry***

Jewelry is one of the best ways to express yourself and improve your self-image as it gives you a sense of uniqueness. Statement bracelets, rings, or necklaces add style and personality to your outfit. These pieces of jewelry are also fun. You can wear jewelry with sentimental value such as heirlooms. These pieces of jewelry allow you to show how much you care about the people around you. Don't wear diamonds and pearls only on special occasions. Wearing expensive jewelry can make you feel special.

- ***Choose the right underwear***

The right underwear can make your outfits look better. You will also feel better because you're comfortable. The wrong underwear can give unnecessary lumps, lines, and other issues under the clothes. You can go to a specialty shop or underwear section of the nearest department store in your area and get assistance from a sales associate.

- ***Pair your clothes with accessories***

Some accessories help you stand out. Some accessories might help you blend in more or hide. For instance, colorful ties can be paired with a grey or white button-up. You can also wear a patterned tie. Hats can be paired with different outfits. There are various kinds of hats that you can put with formal and casual clothes. Summer scarves can be paired with shirts and dresses. Other accessories that you can wear include gloves, sunglasses, and bags.

- ***Change your attitude about your self-image and clothes***

You should dress for success and confidence, especially if you want to improve your self-image. Wearing nice clothes will boost your confidence during interviews or at work. Choose clothes that fit you properly and emphasize your personality goals. You don't have to wear a 3-piece suit or an all-black suit. It's good to dress for success, but you have to add your personality as well. You can pair a plain dress or suit with a pair of bright shoes, a colorful tie, and statement jewelry.

It's also important to accept your imperfection and flaws. Your clothes might be nice, but your self-image will be affected negatively if you focus on what you consider imperfections or flaws. All of us have something we don't like about ourselves. Wearing a dress that shows your strengths will make you feel great about yourself. However, you have to accept your imperfections and flaws. Don't think about what is wrong with your body when you wear clothes. Look at the positive side of things. Think about how the dress you are wearing empowers you. Determine the strengths emphasized by your wardrobes, such as your eyes or legs.

It is also important to recognize outfits that harm your self-image. If you wear sweatshirts and sweatpants when you are feeling down, you should not wear them when you are feeling happy. Your clothes may show what you're feeling right now. You might feel bad if you wear outfits with bad associations.

If you have time and money to spare, you can enroll in a clothing and self-image workshop. A lot of psychologists, wardrobe specialists and nutritionists offer workshops that discuss the link between clothing and self-esteem and self-image. These workshops can help you learn how to dress for your body and how your clothes affect your self-image. Ask local wellness centers if there are clothing and self-image workshops in your area. You can also search for such workshops online.

How to Master Self-Discipline

According to studies, people with a higher level of self-control are happier. Those who have self-discipline spend less time deliberating whether to practice behaviors that can harm their health. They can make positive decisions quickly and easily. People with self-discipline don't allow their feelings or impulses to control them. They make sensible decisions, and because of this, they feel more satisfied and happier. If you want to take full control of your choices and habits, here are some things that you can do to learn and master self-discipline.

- ***Build self-discipline***

Self-discipline is a learned behavior. It requires repetition and daily practice. Self-discipline takes a lot of work, effort, and focus. Maintaining your resolve becomes more difficult as time goes by. The bigger the decision or temptation, the harder it can feel about dealing with other issues that need self-discipline. To prevent this from happening, you should work on improving your self-discipline by practicing every day.

- ***Keep things simple***

Learning a new habit can feel overwhelming at first. To avoid feeling overwhelmed, you should keep things simple. Divide goals into smaller, more manageable steps. Don't try to change everything simultaneously. Do one thing constantly and master self-control while keeping this goal in mind. For instance, you should work out 10 to 15 minutes every day if you want to get in shape.

You should go to bed 10 minutes earlier every night if you want to develop better sleeping habits. Wake up 15 minutes earlier to prepare your lunch if you want to eat a well-balanced diet. Taking baby steps can help you avoid feeling overwhelmed.

Once you have adjusted to these changes, you can take on bigger goals.

- ***Identify your weaknesses***

Everyone has weaknesses. It may be the latest game app or dark chocolate. You should recognize your weaknesses. People often try to cover up setbacks in their lives or pretend that they don't have vulnerabilities. Acknowledging your weaknesses is the first step to conquering them.

- ***Create a backup plan***

An implementation intention is a technique used by psychologists to improve willpower. This technique involves creating a plan to handle a potentially challenging situation that you might face. For example, you are trying to lose weight. However, you have to attend your friend's birthday party, and you know that foods and drinks will be served there.

Before you go, you should tell yourself that you will focus on socializing and drink water instead of eating cakes or pastries. This will give you the self-control and mindset needed for the situation. You won't make sudden decisions that are driven by your emotions.

- ***Get rid of temptations***

Removing the biggest temptations will help increase your self-discipline. For example, don't buy crackers or junk food if you want to lead a healthy lifestyle. Silence your mobile phone and turn off notifications if you want to be more productive. If there are fewer distractions, you will be more focused. This will help you achieve your goals faster.

- ### *Eat healthily and often*

When you are hungry, you get irritated or angry easily. This can affect your willpower. According to studies, low blood sugar weakens resolve and makes a person pessimistic and cranky. When you are hungry, your brain won't be able to function properly. You can't focus, and your self-control is weakened. This can affect various areas of your life, such as your relationships and work. For example, you may lash out at your friend, or you may not finish the presentation you are making. You should eat regular meals and healthy snacks, so you will have the energy needed to do your tasks.

- ### *Have a clear plan to reach your goals*

Having a clear idea of what you want to achieve is important if you want to master self-discipline. You should also understand what success really means to you. If you don't know which path you should take, you will get sidetracked or lose your way easily. When you have a clear plan, you know what step you should take to accomplish your goals.

- ***Move forward***

If you make a mistake, you should forgive yourself. Things don't always go the way you want them to. You will have failures and successes. Accept this fact and keep moving forward.

- ***Don't forget to reward yourself***

When you accomplish your goal, you should reward yourself. You will have something to be happy and excited about. This will motivate you to work harder. Anticipation gives us something to focus on and obsess over. When you finally get what you've always wanted, you can set a new goal. Reward yourself when you accomplish your new goal. Just repeat the process. If you fail, recognize the cause of your failure and move on. Never allow yourself to get wrapped up in anger, disappointment or guilt because these emotions will impede your future progress. Forgive yourself and learn from your mistakes.

Tips to Improve Your Self-esteem

Poor self-esteem can leave you feeling apathetic and unsure of yourself. You might be able to determine some factors that affect how you view yourself. Perhaps you are feeling lonely, or you are being bullied. Regardless of the reason, there are a lot of things that you can do to boost your self-esteem. Here are some of them.

- ***Always remember that nobody's perfect***

You want to be a better person. However, you should also keep in mind that perfection is an impractical goal. Nobody's perfect. Never compare yourself to others. If you do, you will start feeling worthless. Focus on your achievements and goals. Don't measure them against another person's accomplishments. Don't put too much pressure on yourself.

- ***Be good to yourself***

Be good to yourself. If you make a mistake, challenge your negative thoughts. You should talk to yourself in the same manner that you would speak to your friend. It might be hard at first, but you shouldn't give up. Keep practicing, and you will be good at it eventually.

- ***Focus on the things that can be changed***

Don't get hung up on what you can't control. Instead, focus your effort and energy on identifying what's within your control and what you can do about these things.

- ***Celebrate small achievements***

Perhaps you were able to finish your homework 10 minutes earlier than you expected. Maybe you woke up early this morning. Celebrating small achievements is one of the best ways to boost your confidence and feel better about yourself. You should do what brings you happiness.

For example, you love gardening. You can plant in your garden or trim the grass during your free time or day off. Perhaps you love cooking. Get a cookbook or watch a tutorial on how to cook a new dish. If you do things that you love, you are likely to think positively. By having some "me time" every day, you can avoid feeling overwhelmed.

Being considerate and helpful to others will improve your mood as well. Avoid people who tend to trigger negative thinking. Look for those who make you feel great about yourself.

Chapter 9: Taking Action

If there's a goal you want to achieve, you already know that you need to take action to make it a reality. It is easy to read a lot of success techniques, self-help book, and guidance notes. However, these resources will not let you go very far. For instance, nothing good will happen from simply knowing a successful method if you never use it.

You should take action now. While reading is the first step to making the changes in your life, it won't change anything. Changes can only occur once you take action. If you don't act on what you have learned, it is considered as a type of procrastination. Here are reasons why you should take action.

- ***Eliminate methods that don't work***

You will never know if a method works or doesn't work for you if you don't give it a try. Through trial and error, you can eliminate the methods that don't work for you. You will have enough energy and time to focus on perfecting those that work.

- ***Activate information***

Use an inspiring piece of information with practical tips to make tangible changes. For instance, you won't be a confident person right after reading a book on confidence. You have to apply that piece of information to get your desired results. If the book shared tips on how to dress appropriately, you should update your wardrobe.

• ***Take action toward change***

You can't just make one attempt and never try anything again. At first, you have to exert a lot of effort to complete a new action. That new action will eventually turn into a habitual pattern of behavior. Getting started is the most difficult part of taking action. The new action will become second nature to you. If you don't start, it will not become a habit.

• ***Sense of accomplishment***

Taking action gives you a sense of accomplishment. You may have read all those books, but you won't get anything if you don't do something about the information you gathered. Failure to take action might be your way of resisting change and validating procrastination. Change is inevitable, but you don't need to take it negatively. This is your chance to improve your current life.

How to Become More Action-oriented

The first step to becoming more action-oriented is identifying what you should take action on. Determine the areas of your life that need changes. Perhaps your eating habits leave you hungry and sluggish throughout the whole day. Maybe your morning routine decreases your productivity. You have to determine the problem areas of your life so that you can create an effective plan to counter these issues. There will be setbacks, but don't give up.

The next step is identifying the required steps of action. Well-planned actions will give your desired results. Impulsive actions without any direction may lead to failure. You don't want to take the wrong path, so make sure to determine which actions would bring you success. Perhaps your current actions are causing more harm than good. Determine how you are going to replace or change these actions to get your intended results.

You should also prepare yourself to face various possible outcomes. This way, you can increase your chances of making successful changes in your life. Ask yourself some questions to determine how prepared you are.

- *Do you need resources to make your plans a reality?*
- *Do you have access to these resources?*
- *Can you see possible obstacles to your success?*
- *What actions can you take to overcome or prevent these obstacles?*
- *Are you prepared to take action?*

Remember that taking action requires willpower and motivation. You won't get anywhere by just reading a book or any other material you found online. Unless you take action on the information you gain, you won't get anything at all.

Excuses that Prevent People from Taking Action

Excuses prevent you from achieving what you want. Here are the most common excuses that people prevent from taking action.

- ***It's a bad time***

The best time to start is now. Something will always happen like a child or an unexpected bill. You will regret it if you don't start working for your goal as early as now.

- ***Fear***

Successful people also have fears, but they are brave enough to overcome that fear. Fear can motivate you to work harder. If your goal doesn't scare you, you should remove it from your list because you will abandon it. Use fear as your motivation to take on challenges.

- ***Time***

When you say you don't have time, it shows that you don't have full control of your life. If you have important plans, you can turn down invitations. It's okay to do that. Eliminate unnecessary matters that consume a lot of your time. Proper time management will increase your productivity.

- ***Money***

You have to learn how to prioritize. Identify items that are considered needs or wants. Determine areas where you could save money. You can cook homemade meals instead of eating out. Doing so will not only help you save money but also ensure that you're eating healthy.

If your goal inspires other people, you should let them help. A lot of people are willing to donate to a worthwhile cause. If what's offering is valuable and unique, people will be willing to help you. You can seek help from family and friends. Just make sure that you have a good execution strategy and plan so that you can present something to them. You can't expect them to help if you ask for money without any plan. Loans are also an option. Just make sure that you read the terms and conditions of the loan before signing anything.

- ***Age***

Age doesn't matter when you want to set up a business. If you're young, take advantage of your youth. You have health and time. There's no wife, mortgage, or kid to worry about. Your obligations are fewer than that of an adult. What if you're already 50 and have arthritis? Should you give up and never try at all? No! Focus on the process and the people you want to work with. Don't let your age stop you from creating a successful business.

- ***Overwhelmed***

A goal will look so large that you may not have any idea where to start. Focus on the smaller tasks that will help you achieve your goals. For instance, you want to lose 20 pounds in 20 days. You can start by losing 1 pound every day instead of the overall goal. By focusing on daily goals, you will gradually get what you want.

- ***It is too difficult***

It's never easy to reach a goal. If it's that easy, everyone would be living their dream life. If you want something, you have to work for it. Maybe you have to do something you don't particularly like. Maybe you are not a morning person, but you need to get up early to prepare your lunch. If the goal is hard to achieve, it is a good thing because it is a sign that you will not get bored.

- ***Poor self-esteem***

If you believe you are not smart enough to be successful, you won't be. You have to reframe your mindset. If you think that not being successful is who you are, you should change your belief to being successful is who you are. By changing your story and actions, you can change your life.

- ***Fear of failure***

When you want to achieve something, you have to accept that there is a 50/50 chance of succeeding or failing. This percentage is quite good. You need to get used to this fact. Few things have a success rate of 100%. Don't quit and overcome your fear of failure. Don't worry about what other people will say.

Thinking about what others think is an excuse often made by those who tend to quit. The naysayers will validate that tendency. Don't let their negativity hinder you. These people will disapprove your goal because they're not determined enough to pursue their won. When you do achieve your goals, they will praise you.

Positively reframe excuses to gain momentum. Your excuses are just in your head. Once you acknowledge this fact, you can start to write a new story and take a step closer to your goals. You will feel a lot better because you know that you overcame your excuses.

Chapter 10: Emotional Intelligence

Emotional Intelligence (EI) is the ability to understand, identify, and manage your own emotions. It also refers to a person's ability to understand, identify, and influence the emotions of other people. You have to manage your Emotional Intelligence when dealing with failure, change, setbacks, and challenging relationships. The same can be said in receiving or giving feedback, and when you don't have enough resources. Here are the 5 components of EI.

- ***Social skills***

People who are an emotionally intelligent show they respect and care for others. They get along well with other people.

- ***Motivation***

Emotionally intelligent people tend to be extremely motivated. This makes them more optimistic and stronger.

- ***Self-awareness***

When you are self-aware, you know your weaknesses and strengths. You also know how to respond to people and situations.

- ***Empathy***

Those who have compassion and empathy are better at connecting with others.

- ***Self-control***

People with high emotional intelligence can control their emotions. They can keep their emotions in check as needed.

Emotional intelligence is vital in building a well-balanced life. It is significant not only for people who always communicate or interact with others. Emotional intelligence is essential in various areas of life.

- ***Conflict Resolution***

Recognizing people's emotions and understanding their perspective makes it easier to avoid or resolve conflicts. An emotionally intelligent person is also better at negotiation because of their ability to understand the desires and needs of others. After all, it is easier to give others what they want if you can recognize what it is.

- ***Mental Well-being***

A person's mental intelligence affects his outlook on life and attitude. It also helps prevent mood swings and depression as well as alleviate anxiety. When your emotional intelligence is high, you will have a happier outlook on life and a positive attitude.

- ***Physical Health***

Your ability to take care of your body to manage stress can affect your overall wellness. It is also linked to your emotional intelligence. By being aware of your emotional state and your reaction to stress, you will be able to maintain good health and manage stress a lot better.

- ***Leadership***

Your ability to establish stronger bonds with other people and understand what inspires others as well as relationships in a positive way makes you an effective leader. This kind of leader can determine what his people need. This way, their needs can be provided in a manner that promotes workplace satisfaction and better performance. An emotionally intelligent leader can create a stronger team by strategically using the team members' emotional diversity.

- ***Relationships***

If you can perfectly manage and understand your emotions, you can positively communicate your feelings. You're also better able to relate to other people and understand them. Understanding the reactions, needs, and feelings of the people you care about helps you build more fulfilling and stronger relationships.

- ***Success***

High emotional intelligence allows you to be a strong internal motivator. This can reduce procrastination, improve your capability to focus on goals and boost self-confidence. You can also build a better network of support and overcome setbacks. Another benefit of high emotional intelligence is that you will keep trying with a more positive outlook. Your ability to see the long-term and delay gratification affects your ability to be successful.

Emotions play a significant role in the quality of your professional and personal lives. It is more important than the actual measure of your brain intelligence. Also, there is technology and tools that can help expand your knowledge. But nothing can replace your capability to master and manage your emotions as well as the emotions of other people around you.

Signs that You Are Emotionally Intelligent

Here are some of the most common actions that show how emotionally intelligent a person can be.

- ***Demonstrate empathy***

Empathy helps you connect with other people. Someone who shows empathy doesn't label or judge others. It doesn't necessarily mean that they agree with other people's opinion. They strive to understand others, which helps them build more connected and stronger relationships

- ***Knowing when to pause***

An emotionally intelligent person knows when to stop. They think before they act or speak, which saves them from making commitments too fast or being involved in embarrassing situations. Pausing prevents them from making decisions based on temporary emotions.

- ***Ability to focus on your thoughts***

While you don't have full control over the emotions, you feel at a particular moment. You can control your response to those emotions. You need to focus on your thoughts. If you can control your thoughts, you can live in a way that's in line with your values and goals. This is because your emotions are not controlling you.

- ***Praising others***

We all want to be appreciated and acknowledged. When you praise another person, you fulfill that desire and establish trust in the process. You can do this by focusing on the good in other people. By sharing what you are pleased about, you encourage them to be a better person.

- ***Taking criticism as a way to improve yourself***

You don't enjoy negative feedback, but take this as a chance to improve yourself. Even when the feedback is groundless, it helps you know how other people think. When you hear a negative feedback, you should control your emotions. Ask yourself how this feedback can make you better.

- ***Social and self-awareness***

Emotional intelligence starts with social and self-awareness. It's the ability to identify emotions and how they affect you and other people. Social and self-awareness start with reflection. Ask yourself what your emotional strengths and weaknesses are. You should also ask yourself how your current mood affects your decision making and thoughts. Finding answers to these questions can help you gain valuable insights that you can use to your advantage.

- ***Authentic***

Showing authenticity doesn't mean that you have to reveal everything about yourself all the time. It is about saying what you mean and adhering to your principles and values. While not everyone will be grateful to you for sharing your feelings and thoughts, the ones who do will appreciate your authenticity.

- ***Helping others***

Helping other people is one of the best ways to positively influence their emotions. Most people don't care about your past accomplishments. What about the time you are willing to spend to help out or listen? What about your willingness to work together with them? Such actions inspire others to do the same thing and build trust.

You are also willing to provide helpful feedback. Criticism can be reframed as constructive feedback so as not to hurt the recipient's feelings. This way, the person sees the criticism as beneficial instead of harmful.

- ***Willingness to apologize***

Apologizing to someone takes a lot of courage and strength. Your willingness to apologize shows your humility, which is a quality that will draw other people to you. An emotionally intelligent person knows that saying sorry doesn't always mean that they are wrong. It shows that they value their relationship more than their ego.

- ***Ability to avoid emotional sabotage***

An emotionally intelligent person may try to manipulate other people's emotions for some selfish cause. You recognize this fact and avoid emotional sabotage. This also means forgiving others and forgetting what they have done. If you hang on to resentment, you won't find happiness. The person who offended you moves on with his life, but you're just there. You're not giving yourself a chance to heal. By forgiving and forgetting, you're allowing yourself to move forward. Your emotions are not held hostage by other people.

An emotionally intelligent person also keeps his commitments. Some people break a commitment or agreement when they want to. When you keep your word no matter how small or big the commitment is, you will develop a reputation for trustworthiness and reliability.

How to Develop Emotional Intelligence

You can work on your emotional intelligence. Here are some tips on how to improve your EI.

- ***Channel your emotions properly***

You can't control emotions, but you can react to them. Remember that there are only bad and good reactions to emotions. For example, joy can be a bad emotion if it is obtained from hurting other people. It can be a good emotion when shared with your loved ones.

Anger can be a harmful emotion if you react to it negatively and hurt others or yourself in the process. However, anger can be a good emotion if it's used to protect others or yourself and to correct injustices. Managing your emotions is important. You have to recognize what you feel, determine whether or not that is the right emotion for the situation and act accordingly. In other words, you should be able to channel emotions into goal-directed behaviors.

- ***Practice self-awareness***

You can't really master something if you don't know what it really is. When you don't have self-awareness, you will find it hard to manage your emotions. You will be easily influenced by what is happening around you. Since you can't manage your emotions, you won't know where you should go or how you should get there. You can only ask for help from others.

Being self-aware means, you understand yourself as well as your behavior based on what you are doing and your feelings about it. Self-awareness also helps you figure out the things that you don't know regarding yourself.

You might think that it's easy to know what you are doing. However, most people don't even know what they're doing half the time. They are on autopilot. It's important to get rid of distractions from your life. You can turn off your phone once in a while and go out more often. Find a room where you can relax. Video games, TV, internet, and arguing with people online are common forms of distraction that you would do well without.

Make sure to spend some time away from these distractions. For example, you can commute without listening to any podcast or music. You can think about how you are feeling and contemplate life in general. Meditate for at least 10 minutes or deactivate your social media for 1 week.

Distractions are often used to avoid uncomfortable emotions. Eliminating distractions and focusing on your emotions may force you to face scary revelations sometimes. However, eliminating distractions is important because it helps you move forward.

You should also know what you really feel. Once you pay attention to your feelings, you might be surprised. You might realize that you have anger management problems or you are often sad. Perhaps you are suffering from a lot of stress, and your coping mechanism is playing video games all day. It's your only way to distract yourself from stress and anxiety. Don't be quick to judge the emotions that you feel. You might be tempted to ask what's wrong with you. Doing so will make things worse. There's a reason why you are feeling that emotion. Perhaps you don't remember the reason, but don't be so hard on yourself.

Once you know that uncomfortable emotion, you will start to see where your own crazy resides. Maybe you get really irritated when you are interrupted. Perhaps you get angry when the person you are talking to is distracted. By being aware of your emotional bullshit, you can react better against it.

- ***Motivate yourself***

There are instances when you lose yourself completely in a certain activity. You got so immersed in that activity that when you finally snapped out of it, several hours have already passed. Maybe this happens when you're reading a really good book or tending to your garden. You lose your sense of time, but you feel satisfied at the same time. When you get this feeling, it motivates you to keep going.

However, you should not wait for this feeling to happen before you start tending to your garden. You start trimming the shrubs, and that feeling begins to build up. This feeling inspires you to continue. You may want to water the plants or sweep fallen leaves. That feeling builds more. This is called the do something principle. According to the principle, taking action is the cause and effect of motivation. Many people look for inspiration first so that they can take some big action and change their situation. They try to motivate themselves with whatever stimulus they found that week so that they can take action. By next week, however, they have run out of motivation. They are back to square one, and they have to find another source of motivation.

When you need to be inspired, you only have to do something that is slightly related to what you want to achieve, and everything will follow. Your action will lead to motivation, and this motivation will inspire you to take action. For instance, when you don't feel like reading, you can sort your books. The point is that you have to do something.

If you don't really feel like anything inspires you, try to do something. You learn how to play the piano or any other musical instrument, sketch, take dancing lessons, or write a poem. If you don't know how to swim, you can take swimming lessons. You can also volunteer in the community. This way, you can do something and give back to your community at the same time. Observe how you feel during, after, and before the activity. Then, use your emotions as a guide for your future behavior.

There are times when it's not "good emotions" that will motivate you. Sometimes, you feel annoyed when you can't say what you want to convey. However, these feelings may fuel your desire to connect with other people. Use as an opportunity to overcome something that is a bit out of your reach.

- **Don't forget your values**

Infusing emotions with values is important. An emotionally intelligent CEO who is using his skills to motivate employees to sell products manufactured by harming the environment or exploiting other people can't say that his emotional intelligence is a virtue.

Conmen have high emotional intelligence because they understand their emotions as well as that of other people. However, they use that skill to manipulate others for their personal gain. They only care about themselves and gain something at the expense of other people. Things can get ugly when a person values little outside of himself.

You choose what you value, and your emotions will complete those values by motivating your behavior one way or another. If you want to live a happy and fulfilling life, you should know what you value. That is where your emotions will be directed. Knowing what you really value is most likely the most emotionally intelligent ability you can develop.

- **Create healthier relationships by recognizing the emotions of other people**

You can't be considered emotionally intelligent if you can only direct and handle your emotions. The main point of developing and improving emotional intelligence is to cultivate healthier relationships with others. Healthy relationships, whether it is a familial relationship, romantic relationship or friendship, start with respect and recognition of other people's emotional needs. You should empathize and connect with others. Vulnerability, shown through sharing yourself truthfully with others and listening to other people, can help you establish healthier relationships.

Empathizing with others doesn't essentially mean that you have to understand them completely. It means that you have to accept someone as he is even when you don't really understand him. You treat him as his own and value his existence. Moreover, you treat that person's pain as your own pain. In other words, you share that pain without judging him.

Chapter 11: Mindset

Mindset pertains to a person's way of thinking. It's a collection of beliefs and thoughts that shape thought habits, which affect how a person thinks, acts and feels.

People with a growth mindset believe that qualities like intelligence can be learned and improved through hard work and commitment. Those who have a fixed mindset think that qualities are innate and cannot be changed.

Importance of Mindset

A person's mindset plays an integral part in how you deal with life's challenges. For instance, a growth mindset improves your resilience. You are more likely to keep trying when you are facing setbacks. A person with a fixed mindset, on the other hand, is more likely to give up. He tends to seek the approval of other people.

Some people do everything they can to prove their worth. They want to prove that they are smart. They always ask themselves if they will be rejected or accepted by others. A person who has a growth mindset is eager to learn more. They want to discover something new and work hard, deal with challenges, and become a better person. A person with a growth mindset doesn't see failure as a disappointment or failure. They see it as a learning experience, which will help them change and grow.

How Mindsets Form

There are 2 kinds of mindsets in a person's early life. It often develops through his experiences in school or the way he's raised

- **Growth Mindset**

Children who are taught to enjoy challenges, explore, and try new experiences are more likely to have a growth mindset. They don't see errors as setbacks, but a chance to achieve their potential and learn something new. Having this kind of mindset doesn't mean that everyone can become anything they wish to be with enough effort and education.

The growth mindset is all about living up to your possible potential. However, it's impossible to know this potential. No one knows how far a person can go if he sets his mind to it. Someone with a growth mindset believes that the effort he spends on learning and improving his skills is worth the trouble.

- **Fixed Mindset**

Kids who are taught to look smart rather than loving learning tend to have a fixed mindset. They are more concerned about how others see them. They are afraid that they may not meet expectations.

What Kind of Mindset Do You Have?

You have a fixed mindset if you believe that people have a particular amount of intelligence and they can't change it. This kind of mindset is also common in people who believe that there's not much they can do to enhance their basic personality and abilities. These people believe that people can't just acquire talent for music, athletics, art, writing, or other things.

You have a growth mindset if you believe that you can change who you are and what you can expand your knowledge as well as learn new things. People with a growth mindset believe that practicing new skills, studying, and working hard can help them develop new abilities and talents.

Is it Possible to Change Your Mindset?

People who have a fixed mindset may disagree that it's possible to change one's mindset. What you need to remember is that people can change their mindsets. You can take steps to make sure that your child develops a growth mindset. This can be done by praising efforts instead of focusing only on results. Praise your child for his hard work on his homework and say what you like the most about his efforts instead of telling him that he's smart. If you focus on the process instead of the result, you can help your child understand that his hard work, dedication, and efforts can lead to growth, learning, and change now and in the future.

Chapter 12: Concentration

Being able to keep your attention on what you're doing can be difficult, especially in today's age of information overload. Americans have presented about 100,500 words and 34 GB of information every day. Office workers are disrupted every 11 minutes, but it takes about 25 minutes to resume the task they were doing before the disruption. It's not really surprising that our ability to concentrate is fading due to these distractions.

The ability to concentrate starts at an early age also contributes to your success. There are various factors during your adolescence and childhood that can impair or improve the development of skills that allow you to concentrate for extended periods. Preschoolers who are capable of concentrating and persisting on a task are 50% more likely to finish college.

According to research, farsighted kindergartners and preschoolers often find it difficult to pay attention. Due to this problem, they might be left behind in lessons. Binge drinking is believed to disrupt normal brain growth. Heavy consumption of alcohol may affect a person's ability to do well in sports and school. Some steps can be taken to improve your concentration. Here are some of them.

- **Train your brain**

Brain training methods, video games, and problem-solving exercises could have a negative or positive effect on your concentration. The effect varies from one person to another. Solving crosswords often can help improve your concentration and attention. According to recent research, people who do word puzzles frequently have better brain function than those who don't. There is a direct link between how often people do word puzzles and the accuracy and speed of performance on tasks that assess attention, reasoning, and memory.

According to a research, the kind of brain training you're doing to improve your attention and memory is important. Two brain-training methods were compared. These methods were the complex span and the dual n-back. Participants who did the dual n-back training method showed a 30% improvement in their memory. This figure is almost double the improvement made by the participants who practiced the complex span training method.

Dual n-back is actually a memory sequence exam where participants need to remember a series of visual and auditory that is updated constantly. Researchers found out that playing video games changed the brain regions that control attention and visuospatial skills and improve their function.

- **Add greenery to your surroundings**

Adding some greenery to your surroundings can help increase your concentration level at work. According to research, exposure to the natural environment may benefit a child's brain development. A study revealed that kids aged 4 to 7 years old who were exposed to green surroundings around their homes scored higher on attention tests. This shows how important expanding green areas can be.

Children are not the only ones who can benefit from exposure to greenery. Research has shown that looking at greenery can increase productivity and productivity in the workplace and college. In one study, students were made to do a simple task and allowed to take a break for 40 seconds midway through to see either a green meadow roof or bare concrete roof. Those who glanced at the meadow green roof showed higher concentration levels and made fewer errors than those who watched the bare concrete roof.

In another study, a bare office that was decorated with plants observed an increase in the productivity of employees by 15%. The presence of plants enhanced concentration, workplace satisfaction, and perceived air quality. According to researchers, plants may be helpful because an office with greenery promotes work engagement by making the employees more physically, cognitively, and emotionally involved in their job.

Although you may not have an office decorated with plants or a rooftop garden, you can improve your concentration levels by eating lunch in the park every day or relaxing outside.

- **Reorganize your environment**

Your environment affects your concentration levels. By tidying your desk or organizing your home, your mind will feel more orderly and free. You will also be able to think more clearly and focus on the task at hand. Design your desk to boost your productivity. It doesn't matter whether you can design your desk with only a few personal trinkets or you have complete control over the design of your desk. Having control over your work environment can have a positive effect on your productivity.

One study compared employees who performed various tasks in an office embellished with photos and plants, an office that allowed employees to design their workspace and a functional and bare office. Workers who were allowed to design their workspace were 32% more productive than employees at a functional and bare office. Employees who worked in an office embellished with photos and plants were 17% more productive than those at a bare office.

Playing nature sounds could improve your concentration, as well. Researchers shared that playing nature sounds, such as flowing water could improve cognitive abilities. You can also try listening to Baroque, classical music. A study about the work-life of radiologists discovered that listening to this kind of music improved job satisfaction and mood. It also potentially enhanced diagnostic efficiency, productivity, and accuracy.

You can inhale rosemary aroma to relax and improve your concentration. According to research, exposure to rosemary fragrance may boost the accuracy and speed of cognitive performance.

- **Improve your overall well-being**

Maintaining weight, exercise, and dietary choices can contribute to your concentration levels and proper functioning. For instance, skipping breakfast will affect your ability to concentrate. By lunchtime, you won't be able to do your tasks properly due to your hunger. Your hunger pangs will disturb you and ruin your concentration.

It is important to stay active and look after your overall well-being. Some foods may help boost your concentration. Avocados, chocolate, and walnuts are good additions to your diet. Walnuts may help improve your performance on cognitive function tests like those that assess information processing speed, concentration, and memory.

Eating 1 avocado daily may help boost cognitive function due to increased lutein levels in the brain and eye. Researchers discovered that eating avocado every day can help improve cognitive skills such as attention, speed, and memory.

Chocolate is packed with flavonols, compounds with neuroprotective properties. The flavanols in chocolate or cocoa beans may help enhance working memory, attention, and cognitive processing speed when consumed for 5 days to 3 months.

Exercise can help improve your concentration, as well. Research shared that those who practice sports can do better on cognitive activities than those who have poor physical health. People who are in good physical condition can perform better than those who lead a sedentary lifestyle when it comes to tasks that test sustained attention.

In one study, older participants said that exercise helped improved their brain function. Those who exercised for 75 to 225 minutes every week showed higher concentration levels than those who did not. If you don't like any vigorous exercise, you can try yoga. Practicing mindfulness meditation and Hatha yoga for 25 minutes every day can help improve the areas of the brain that are linked to goal-directed behavior. This allows you to focus more easily.

You should also check and maintain your weight. Studies found a link between improved concentration and memory and weight loss. Type II diabetes, high blood pressure, and sleep apnea might harm the brain. This is why it is important to maintain a healthy weight. It will not only help you avoid various health problems. You can also prevent cognitive issues from developing.

- **It's okay to take a break**

People with high working memory ability are lucky because it will be easy for them to ignore distractions and stay focused on their tasks. For those who are not, it's difficult to tune out background distractions. You don't need to endure it. It is okay to take a break from time to time. Doing so will actually improve your capability to concentrate. You can take a break from social media, email, and phone notifications.

Control the times you have to log in to your email. You can also batch messages and read them according to importance. These simple strategies can help boost your productivity. According to a study, those who read emails all day were in a constant state of high alert. Their heart rate was also high. When they didn't access email for 5 days, their heart rate resumed to a variable one. Taking a break from emails significantly improves focus and concentration and reduces stress.

Cell phone notifications can divert your attention and ruin your ability to focus on a task. It doesn't really matter whether you're alerted to an incoming call or text by a trendy ringtone, alarm or vibration. Cell phone notifications are a distraction that you should get rid of, especially if you have to finish something. Notifications may be short in duration, but they tend to set off thoughts that are irrelevant to the task. If you have to stay focused because you have a presentation to finish, you can either set your phone to silent, put it away where you can't see it or turn it off.

You should take a break from social media as well. Although you're curious about the latest happenings in your social media, you should hold back. Using social media during work hours can have negative consequences. About 2.8 billion people in the world use social media. Many of them use social media during work hours for personal reasons. This practice hurts concentration and work performance. It can also affect the company's well-being. Fight the urge to access social media. If you really want to know what happening in your friends' lives, you can use social media after you have finished your tasks and once you're at home without anything to do.

Work breaks can boost your productivity as well. You can take a mid-morning break in order to replenish your motivation, concentration, and energy. Do something you like. It would make your break more relaxing. You will also resume your work more focused than before. Frequent short breaks also promote recovery.

You can take a break earlier in the day and do your preferred activities. Doing so leads to better job satisfaction and health.

People who take breaks also experience reduced back pain, eyestrain, and fewer headaches after their break.

Tips to Improve Your Memory

Memories play an important role in your identity. This is why memory loss that is associated with age can mean losing one's sense of self. Some people don't experience any memory loss regardless of age, but others lose it over time. Genes and lifestyle choices contribute to how intact your memories remain.

For instance, exercising regularly, following a healthy diet, and regulating your blood sugar levels, cholesterol, and blood pressure can help protect memory. The brain can continuously change and adapt. It can create new neural connections and cells if it's given the right stimuli. Neuroplasticity pertains to the ability of the brain to grow, change, and improve. Your habits affect the functioning of your brain. Here are some of the best ways to improve your brain's retention and recall.

- **Resistance training and aerobic activity**

Staying active is important to keep your memory sharp. Exercise boosts oxygen levels in the brain, reduces stress hormones, improves the effects of beneficial brain chemicals, and reduces the risk of diabetes and cardiovascular disease. People aged 50 years old and above can benefit from resistance training and aerobic activity. Exercising promotes neuroplasticity of specific structures in the brain that improve cognitive function.

Include at least 45 minutes of moderate-intensity resistance training and aerobic exercise in your workout session. Research suggests that if you wish to remember what you've just learned, exercising 4 hours later would give you the best results. People who worked out 4 hours were better at remembering information than those who exercised right away. They remembered what they learned even after 2 days have passed.

- **It's fine to take a nap**

You can take a nap for 1 hour to boost your cognitive skills. Adults should get 7 to 9 hours of sleep every night. Sleep helps solidify short-term and long-term memory. If you get enough sleep, you will be able to perform and retain information better. If you lack sleep, your brain will have a hard time forming new memories.

In one study, participants who didn't sleep between learning sessions were only able to remember 7.5 words on a memory test. Those who took a nap were able to remember 10 to 16 words. The research revealed that those who take longer naps, or shorter naps, or didn't nap at all show a decline in their mental abilities. By taking a nap, you will be better prepared to do your tasks.

- **Relax**

Stress damages the hippocampus, which can cause memory loss. It also destroys brain cells. You need to manage stress before it causes irreparable harm to your physical and mental health. Listening to your favorite music and meditation may help reduce stress and reverse early memory loss in people who are showing signs of cognitive decline.

A study revealed that listening to music and meditation for 3 months improved the objective cognitive performance and subjective memory function of the participants. These gains were still present 3 months after the program. Twenty-five minutes of Hatha yoga and mindfulness meditation every day can enhance brain function, cognitive abilities, and mood.

You can also use your photography or doodling hobby to improve your ability to remember. One study discovered that doodling while doing a mundane task, improved the participants' memory recall by 29%. Another study showed that taking photos improved the performance of the participants in visual memory tasks.

- **Follow a healthy and brain-boosting diet**

Avoiding the wrong foods and eating the right ones can help fuel the brain and keep it healthy. The Mediterranean diet is among the healthiest diets as it requires you to consume legumes, lean protein, fruits, whole grains, vegetables, beans, and healthy fats like nuts, fish, and olive oil. This kind of diet may protect you against cognitive decline. According to research, the Mediterranean diet helps you live longer and prevents chronic illnesses. It's also associated with improved concentration and memory. Consuming extra-virgin olive oil is a major component of this diet and has been found to protect against cognitive decline.

The Ketogenic diet is also popular due to weight loss claims and various health benefits. This kind of diet is high in fat and low in carbs. The Ketogenic diet requires you to drastically reduce your consumption of carbs and replace them with fat. This puts the body into ketosis, a metabolic state that improves the body's fat-burning ability. Fat is burned for energy. Ketones are created from fat in your liver, and this is what provides energy to the brain. Research in older animals revealed that this kind of diet maintains brain function, improves memory, and increases an animal's lifespan.

If you are looking for foods that are known as memory boosters, here are some of them.

- o **Blueberry concentrate** – It improves working memory, brain function as well as blood flow to your brain. These benefits are particularly beneficial when you are taking cognitive tests.

- **Walnut** – It's linked to improved performance during cognitive function tests for concentration, information processing speed, and memory.
  - **Spinach and kale** – These vegetables contain lutein, which may boost memory and learning and fight against cognitive aging.
  - **Peppermint tea** – It is more effective in improving alertness as well as working and long-term memory than chamomile.
  - **Cinnamon** – It may protect against Alzheimer's disease and cognitive impairment as well as promote memory improvement.
  - **Caffeine** – Drinking 5 cups of coffee every day helped reverse memory impairment in mice suffering from symptoms of Alzheimer's disease.

- **Use mnemonic devices**

Although brain-training programs may improve your performance, they don't really boost intelligence, cognitive abilities, and memory. Mnemonic devices can help you learn to remember and encode important information. If you need to buy your groceries, mnemonic devices can help you remember what you need to get at the grocery store.

Mnemonic devices are particularly beneficial when you need to remember the names of many people. These devices help you connect the information you want to remember with a sentence, word, or image. You memorize information in a manner that makes you remember it easily. That piece of information also lasts in your brain longer. Here are some of the most common mnemonic devices.

- o **Acronyms** – You can use acronyms to remember anything, such as your shopping list or the content of your reviewer. For instance, you can use the acronym TEA to help you remember that you need to buy tissues, eggs, and apples from the store.
- o **Method of loci** – You have to visualize items that you want to remember and a familiar route. It will be easier to remember these items by associating concepts or words with one of the routes along the way.
- o **Rhymes** – Rhymes help you remember information like the number of days there are in January.
- o **Imagery** – Imagery helps you recall pairs of words like green grass and yellow sun. Remembering a specific image enables you to recall information that you linked to that image.
- o **Chunking** – Chunking is all about breaking down a large piece of information into smaller pieces of information. This way, it will be easier to recall the information.

By exercising your brain more often, your ability to process and recall information will definitely improve.

How Meditation Boosts Concentration

The brain is not designed for multitasking. If the brain is forced to switch quickly from one task to the next, your concentration level will drop every time you try to resume a task. Meditation helps improve mental focus by allowing you to recover from distractions. Paying attention to your breathing every time your mind wanders during meditation can help boost the neural circuitry of the brain. When you notice that you are distracted by phone notifications, you will be able to resume whatever you are doing much more quickly. If you can't focus at work, you can take a quick meditation break to restore your concentration.

Meditation is also beneficial to those who have ADD or Attention Deficit Disorder. It can help treat depression and anxiety. As such, researchers have started to explore the possibility of using meditation to treat Attention Deficit Disorder. In a study, researchers discovered that a room of children who have special needs became more focused and calmer when they learned a breathing practice.

Meditation also helps you deal with stress. According to research, meditation allows the amygdala to be quieter. The amygdala is the part of the brain that reacts to stress. This could help you deal with high-pressure situations. You can also avoid being controlled by emotional triggers.

What Kind of Meditation is Right for You?

Meditation improves awareness and relaxation. Mental health experts, educators, and spiritual leaders have developed various forms of meditation. This means that there is a type of meditation that fits your lifestyle and personality. By meditating, you can improve your emotional health and physical wellbeing. There is actually no "right" form of meditation, so you can try different styles until you find one that works for you. Here are some of the best types of meditation.

- **Progressive relaxation**

Also known as body scan meditation, progressive relaxation motivates you to scan your body for tension areas and release this tension. You start at one end of your body like your feet. This form of meditation may require you to tense and relax your muscles. Other forms of body scan meditation require you to imagine a wave drifting over your body to discharge tension.

Progressive relaxation may alleviate chronic pain. It helps promote feelings of relaxation and calmness. This kind of meditation gradually relaxes the body, so you can practice it to help you sleep better.

- **Zen meditation**

Also called Zazen, Zen meditation involves specific poses and steps. This is why many practitioners of Zen meditation study under a capable teacher. You have to find a comfortable pose and focus on your breathing. Zen meditation also requires you to observe your thoughts without prejudice or judgment.

- **Loving-kindness meditation**

Loving-kindness meditation aims to nurture an attitude of kindness and love toward everything. It's also called Metta meditation and is suitable for most people. This form of meditation opens your mind to getting loving kindness. You are required to send messages loving kindness to your loved ones, to the world, and specific individuals. Repeat this message many times until you feel an attitude of kindness and love toward everything.

This form of meditation is beneficial for those affected by disappointment, anger, interpersonal conflict, and resentment. It improves positive emotions and may help reduce anxiety, PTSD, and depression.

- **Mindfulness meditation**

Mindfulness meditation promotes awareness of your present surroundings without judgment. Instead of thinking about how annoying a long wait is, you will simply notice the wait without forming any opinion or judgment. You can do mindfulness meditation almost anywhere. For instance, you can pay attention to your surroundings while waiting in line at a supermarket. You might calmly notice the smells, sounds, and sights you experience. Mindfulness is involved in almost all types of meditation. Breath awareness allows you to be more conscious of your breathing. Progressive relaxation locates tension areas in the body.

Mindfulness is a common theme in different types of meditation, so it has been comprehensively studied. According to research, mindfulness can improve memory, relationship satisfaction, and focus, decrease fixation on unconstructive emotions, and reduce impulsive actions.

- **Transcendental Meditation**

This type of meditation aims to help you rise above your current state of being. It's a spiritual type of meditation where you stay seated and respire slowly. You focus on a repeated or mantra. Your teacher determines the word or series of words based on various factors like the year you were born. Those who practice this kind of meditation report improved mindfulness and spiritual experiences.

A more contemporary version allows you to pick your mantra, but this is not exactly transcendental meditation.

- **Kundalini yoga**

This is a physically active type of meditation that combines movements with mantras and deep breathing. You can either enroll in a Kundalini yoga class or study under a teacher. However, you can also learn the mantras and postures at home.

Kundalini yoga can help reduce pain as well as improve physical strength and mental health by alleviating depression and anxiety.

- **Breath awareness meditation**

This type of meditation promotes mindful breathing by breathing deeply and slowly. You can either focus on your breaths or count your breaths. Your goal is to focus on breathing alone and ignore other thoughts. Breath awareness meditation helps reduce anxiety, improve concentration, and promote emotional flexibility.

Different meditative disciplines focus on promoting slower breathing, improved acceptance, and heightened awareness. Meditation doesn't require you to focus on the results. Being too fixated on the results can trigger feelings of anxiety. Most studies show that meditation can produce results quickly. Research about meditation usually observes practitioners for months or weeks. A lot of practitioners report immediate improvements after a meditation session.

You may feel more accommodating, relaxed, and less stressed during meditation. With practice, you will continue experiencing such emotions outside of your meditation classes.

How Often Should You Meditate?

There's actually no right or wrong answer to this question. Meditating at the same time every day will make meditation a daily habit you can't do without. You can try 1 meditation session every day. If you love the results, you can do more sessions such as twice per day.

If you're new to meditation, you may want to enroll in meditation classes. Doing so will make it easier for you to adjust to a new routine. When you're finally there, enjoy the moment. Meditation focuses on the moment, so you shouldn't be fixated on the outcome. Don't judge whether the session is right or wrong. Just stay in that moment and don't get distracted.

It's not easy to master meditation, but this endeavor is not completely impossible. You may feel angry and frustrated when you first try to meditate. Regardless of your immediate reaction, you should persevere. If you are willing to try different meditation techniques, you will definitely discover the right one that suits your needs.

Yoga to Improve Concentration

Different yoga styles combine breathing techniques, meditation, and physical postures. Yoga has become a popular form of exercise based on poses that improve well-being and focus. Yoga has long been known to help people achieve and physical-mental balance. The Yoga Sutra is a 2,000 year-old dissertation about yogic philosophy written by Patanjali, an Indian sage. It's the earliest written documentation of yoga. The Yoga Sutra is a handbook on how to control the emotions, grow spiritually, and master the mind. It is among the oldest texts existing and offers the framework for modern yoga.

Yogic tradition followers and practitioners in India focused not on fitness, but other practices like increasing spiritual energy through mental focus and breathing techniques. The tradition became more popular in the West in the late 19th century. Postural yoga gained popularity in India and the West during the 1920s and 1930s.

Yoga frequently uses the image of a tree with fruits, blossoms, branches, roots, and trunk to guide sessions and communicate its spiritual message. Each yoga branch has a different focus and characteristics. Here are the 6 branches of yoga.

- **Karma Yoga** – Karma yoga strives to build a future that is free from self-interest and pessimism.

- o **Hatha Yoga** – Hatha yoga is the mental and physical branch aimed to prime the mind and body.
- o **Bhakti Yoga** – Bhakti yoga strives to build the path of devotion and promote open-mindedness and acceptance. It also aims to create a positive manner to convey emotions.
- o **Tantra Yoga** – Tantra yoga is the path of ceremony or ritual. It's the pathway of a relationship's consummation.
- o **Raja Yoga** – Raja yoga involves strict observance of the 8 limbs of yoga, a sequence of disciplinary steps.
- o **Jnana Yoga** – Jnana yoga is all about wisdom. Practitioners develop intellect through study.

Having a specific goal can help you choose which branch you should follow. Yoga teaches that chakras are the main points of the physical body, thoughts, emotions, and energy. Yogic teachers say that chakras determine how a person experiences reality through levels of fear or confidence, emotional reactions, physical symptoms, and aversions or desires. When the energy is blocked in chakras, it is believed to cause emotional, physical, or mental imbalances that manifest in various signs such as poor digestion, apprehension, and exhaustion.

Practitioners of yoga use asanas to stimulate imbalanced chakras and free energy. Asanas are the physical poses in Hatha yoga. The 7 major chakras include the following:

- o **Ajna**

The third-eye chakra or command pertains to a meeting point between 2 energetic streams inside the body. The Ajna chakra is associated with the pituitary gland that drives development and growth. Ajna symbolizes the colors deep blue, violet or indigo. Traditional practitioners of yoga, however, describe Ajna as white.

- o **Sahasrara**

Sahasrara is linked to matters of physical death and inner wisdom. The crown or thousand-petaled chakra stands for the state of consciousness. It can be found at the crown of your head. This chakra is represented by the colors violet or white.

- o **Manipura**

The navel or jewel city chakra is associated with the digestive system, anxiety, personal power, forming opinions, fear, and tendency towards developing an introverted personality. The yellow color represents it.

o **Muladhara**

The root chakra or root support is believed to contain the natural urges associated with sleep, survival, food, and sex. It's located at the base of your spine. This chakra is also believed to be the source of fear and avoidance.

o **Vishuddha**

The throat or especially pure charka is considered to be the home of metabolism, speed, and hearing. It is represented by the color blue or red.

o **Anahata**

The heart or unstruck chakra is linked to compassion, complex emotions, unconditional love, equilibrium, well-being, tenderness, and rejection. The colors pink and green represent Anahata.

o **Svadhishthana**

Svadhishthana or the pelvic chakra is believed to be the home of the adrenal gland, reproductive organs, and genitourinary system.

Types of Yoga

There are different styles of yoga, so you will definitely find something that suits your needs. Modern yoga focuses on breathing, strength, exercise, and flexibility. It also helps boost concentration and physical well-being. Here are the modern styles of yoga.

- **Iyengar yoga**

Iyengar yoga is all about identifying the right alignment in every pose. This is done by using different props like chairs, bolsters, blocks, straps, and blankets.

- **Bikram yoga**

Bikram yoga is also called hot yoga. It is held in an artificially heated room. The humidity level in the room is 40%, and the temperature is almost 105°. Bikram yoga is composed of a series of 2 breathing exercises and 26 poses.

- **Ashtanga yoga**

Ashtanga yoga gained popularity in the 1970s. It makes use of ancient yoga teachings and applies 6 established series of poses that quickly connect each movement to breathe.

- **Hatha yoga**

Hatha yoga introduces you to the fundamental yoga poses.

- **Kundalini yoga**

Kundalini yoga is a form of meditation that helps you release built-up energy. Classes usually start with chanting and end with singing. Meditation, asana, and pranayama are featured in between classes to create an inevitable result.

- o **Yin**

Yin is also known as Taoist yoga. It's a meditative yoga practice that helps release tension in joints such as the hips, ankles, neck, back, shoulders, and knees. Postures in yin yoga are passive.

- o **Jivamukti yoga**

Jivamukti yoga includes practices that concentrate on the quick flow between postures. It also includes spiritual teachings. This kind of yoga can be tiring. Classes have themes that are explored through chanting, yoga scripture, music, meditation, pranayama, and asana.

- o **Restorative yoga**

Restorative yoga is perfect for those who want to relax. You do 4 or 5 poses using bolsters, blankets or other props to achieve a state of deep relaxation. Since you are using props, you don't have to exert any effort in maintaining the pose.

- o **Kripalu yoga**

Kripalu yoga teaches you how to learn from, know, and accept the body. Classes usually start with gentle stretches and breathing exercises. These poses are followed by individual poses and then relaxation.

o **Viniyoga**

Teachers of Viniyoga tend to be experts in yoga therapy and anatomy. Anyone can practice viniyoga regardless of their physical ability.

o **Sivananda**

Sivananda uses the 12 fundamental asanas, savasana poses, and sun salutations. It also includes proper breathing, positive thinking, relaxation, exercise, and diet to create a healthy yogic lifestyle.

o **Prenatal yoga**

Prenatal yoga involves doing poses designed for pregnant women. This kind of yoga can help them get back onto shape after they give birth.

Asanas that Improve Concentration

- **Tadasana**

Tadasana, also known as the Mountain Pose, can be done anytime. If you are following it up with other poses, your stomach should be empty, or there should be a gap of 1 to 3 hours from the last meal. You should hold this pose for 10 to 20 seconds. Tadasana offers several benefits such as increasing awareness, strengthening legs, improving posture, and balancing breathing. It also firms the buttocks and abdomen. Tadasana improves the flexibility of the spine as well as reduces pain and tension in the body.

- **Natarajasana**

Natarajasana is named after Lord Shiva's dancing avatar – Nataraja. It is also known as the Dancer Pose. This pose is best practiced daily early in the morning. Hold this posture for 15 to 30 seconds. It must be done before any meal. Natarajasana improves metabolism and digestion, which helps you lose weight. It also strengthens ankles, chest, and thighs. Natarajasana makes your body more flexible. It also improves endurance and blood flow as well as helps reduce stress and treat depression.

- **Vrikshasana**

Vrikshasana, also known as the Tree Pose, improves stability in the legs. It also builds self-esteem and confidence, improves balance, stretches the whole body, increases stamina, treats numbness, and calms the nervous system. The pose is reminiscent of a tree. You don't have to close your eyes while doing this pose. Practice this pose early in the day on an empty stomach. You need to keep your eye open while doing this pose to maintain balance. Hold the pose for 1 minute.

- **Garudasana**

Garudasana is named after Lord Vishnu's vehicle and the king of birds – Garuda. It's also known as the Eagle Pose. Garudasana is best practiced in the morning. Hold the posture for 10 to 30 seconds. It should be practiced on an empty stomach. Garudasana improves neuromuscular coordination, makes the legs and hips more flexible, balances the body, and makes the muscles of the legs stronger. This pose also helps eliminate urinal problems, corrects postural issues, and prevents asthma.

- **Ustrasana**

Ustrasana is a backward bend that looks like the posture of a camel when it sits. It is also called the Camel Pose and is best practiced in the morning on clean bowels and an empty stomach. You can practice it in the evening as well. Just make sure to eat your meals 4 to 6 hours before doing this pose. Hold Ustrasana for 30 to 60 seconds. This pose improves posture, stretches and strengthens shoulders and back as well as alleviates backache. It also improves digestion, excretion, respiration, and endocrine glands. Ustrasana balances and heals the chakras and alleviates menstrual discomfort.

- **Bakasana**

Bakasana looks like a crane's posture when performed. It is also called the Crane Pose. The crane symbolizes longevity and happiness in many cultures. This pose can be practiced in the evening or the morning on an empty stomach. Hold the pose for 30 to 60 seconds. If you want to practice this pose in the evening, you should do it 4 to 6 hours after your last meal. Bakasana enhances endurance, and mental strength improves the spine's flexibility and tones the abdominal muscles. It can also help you develop positive thinking and improved body awareness. This pose helps eliminate anxiety and tension as well as enhances mind-body coordination.

- **Paschimottanasana**

Paschimottanasana is also known as Seated Forward Bend. It's a forward bend that is focused on the back of the body. This pose calms the mind, reduces constipation, treats headache and stomach pain, boosts appetite, energizes the body, and strengthens the hip bones. It should be practiced on clean bowels and empty stomach in the morning. If you want to practice this pose in the evening, you should do it after a gap of 4 to 6 hours from your last meal. Hold the pose for 30 to 60 seconds.

Yoga focuses on the present. According to studies, practicing yoga on a regular basis improves reaction time, IQ scores, coordination, and memory. Practitioners of transcendental meditation show the ability to acquire and remember information and solve problems better. This is most likely because they are less preoccupied with their thoughts. Yoga can also help shift the balance from the fight-or-flight response or sympathetic nervous system to the restorative and calming parasympathetic nervous system. The latter lowers heart rate, blood pressure, and breathing. It also improves blood flow to the reproductive organs and intestines. Yoga offers many benefits, so there is no reason why you shouldn't try it.

Chapter 13: Achieve Success

The common belief is that you have to suffer more and work harder than anyone else if you want to succeed. That is partially true. Many successful people had actually discovered something great when they understood that working hard was a waste of energy and time. Here are the most important factors to consider when you are aiming for success.

- ***Self-work***

If you improve yourself 5 times as hard as you develop external elements, you will feel that you're moving 5 times faster than you want. Your hard work is focused on replacing old habits and routines with ones successful people have. Changing your habits on purpose will help you change the outcome you get, the way you see yourself, and the value you offer.

For example, you want to become a notable martial artist. You could train like Bruce Lee every day to achieve that. If you want to boost your sales, you could integrate the same habits and routines that have helped your competitors increase their sales.

Start making changes as early as today and get great results as soon as possible. You only need to replace self-limiting beliefs and old habits with more positive and productive ones.

- ***Purpose***

Perhaps you have been working for your company for so long that you already forgot why you applied to them. People who consider themselves a failure lack one thing, and that is a purpose. They have no idea which path or direction they should take. Maybe they don't even have any idea why they are doing that particular task or activity. They pursue only short-term satisfactions such as food. These people function using only their animal side, so they're not capable of doing personal analysis or long-term thinking.

If you don't know your purpose, you will realize that you are doing something without knowing why you're doing it in the first place. Although momentum is a good thing, it can also be one of the factors that are simply a waste of time. When you take action, remember that you have to keep on doing it forever unless an external or internal factor reminds you to begin doing something else.

Perhaps you are developing something without knowing what the result would be. It may take days or hours of hard work to understand that you shouldn't be doing what you are doing right now. This is particularly true when you want to accomplish your goals. You should be someone who plans ahead and takes purposeful actions.

- ***Belief***

If you don't think you can accomplish your goal, you'll never become successful even if you work day and night. You have to get rid of any mental barrier you have. By doing so, you will get what you have always wanted. If you don't believe that you can get it, you will continue making distractions and excuses. It feels scary or uncomfortable to be someone you don't think you can be. You might feel uneasy about the thought of having something you don't believe you're prepared to have. By removing negative beliefs or ideas about what you can become and what you can have, your life would change a life.

These factors require focus and hard work, but they can help you avoid a lot of stress and frustration. Here are some tips on how to get what you want in life.

- ***Seek knowledge***

By focusing on the excitement of experimenting, discovery, improving, and exploring, you will remain motivated. If you are just focused on the results, your motivation will be gone the moment you encounter a problem. In other words, you should focus on the journey. Think about what you're learning and what can be improved.

- ***Challenge yourself***

Your actions may fail to bring your desired results, so you choose not to partake in any difficult situation. You wait for an opportunity or the right timing while feeling depressed about your lack of success. Challenge yourself and do what you've always wanted to do even if you're scared.

- ***Be fully committed***

Determine how important your goal is for you and what you're willing to sacrifice to get it. By staying committed to your goal, you will remain motivated as well. Don't forget to make the journey exciting. If you stay serious all the time, you will lose your motivation and become stuck once more.

- ***Find ways to avoid burnout***

Avoid burnout by observing yourself. If you notice signs of tiredness, you should take a break. Include fun time and relaxation in your weekly calendar to allow your mind and body to rest. Do something logical and creative and try different tasks. You can also change locations. Meditation is also a good option. Close your eyes and take deep breaths. Use this chance to focus on a single thing for 5 minutes.

- ***Use imagination***

Using your imagination is one of the best ways to eliminate negative thoughts. When you are in a difficult situation, you should be more energetic. For example, saying that you hate your work repeatedly will evoke negative feelings. Find something new to learn from your job. Try to say and think about positive things only for 3 days. You will benefit from the positive vibes it will bring.

- ***Eliminate distractions and stagnating thoughts***

Distractions will always come your way. Focus on what's really important. Create a list of tasks that are just a waste of your precious time. Hold yourself responsible not to do these tasks. Your thoughts also affect your emotions, and your emotions affect how you see your job. You can choose to focus on thoughts that will help you move forward, such as trying new things or on thoughts that make you emotionally trapped like doubts and fears.

- ***Plan***

Creating a plan will also help you avoid distractions. You have to know how, when, and what in order to create a plan that suits your needs. What did you learn today? Assess how each day passed by what you learned and modify the areas that can be improved.

- ***Avoid relying on others***

Don't expect other people to do what you need to do. You're the only one who can accomplish your goals.

Sometimes, you lack motivation not because you don't have goals or you are lazy. Motivation may come from your curiosity about how faster and better you can get. Curiosity will help you move forward, as well.

Exercises to Develop Mental Toughness

Mental toughness requires commitment, willpower, and hard work. It is about devoting your energy and time to self-improvement and establishing healthy habits. True mental toughness becomes more apparent when you are in a difficult situation. Developing skills that improve your mental toughness is one of the best ways to prepare for the challenges and setbacks that may come your way. Here are some exercises that can help boost your mental toughness.

- ***Spend mental energy sensibly***

You don't want to waste your mental energy on things you cannot control. The less you think about issues you cannot solve, the more energy you will have to spare for your creative endeavors. For example, worrying about the latest weather forecast won't help you at all. It will not prevent a storm headed your way, but you can prepare for it. You can prepare flashlights and batteries, canned goods, cash, and clothes.

Focus on what's within your control. Use your mental energy on productive activities such as setting goals and solving problems. By spending your mental energy sensibly every day, it will become second nature to you.

- ### *Think of productive thoughts*

If you're aware of your thinking habits, it will be easier to improve your resilience. Pessimistic thoughts like you can't do anything right prevent you from achieving your full potential. Catch pessimistic thoughts before they influence your behavior. Replace negative thoughts with more productive ones. Productive thoughts should be realistic. You can say that you have some weaknesses, but you also have a lot of strengths. Constant monitoring is required when you are aiming to change your thoughts. The process can help you become the best version of yourself.

- ### *Reflect upon your progress every day*

Your busy schedule may prevent you from doing a quiet reflection. However, you should allocate enough time to reflect on your progress every day. What have you learned about your emotions, behavior, and thoughts? What do you want to accomplish or improve tomorrow?

- ***Assess your core beliefs***

Core beliefs mostly depend on your past experiences. These beliefs influence your behavior, emotions, and thoughts. However, your core beliefs might be unproductive and inaccurate. If you think that you will never succeed, you may not be motivated to apply for a new job. You may not do your best during job interviews. Determine and assess your core beliefs. Changing core beliefs requires hard work and focused intention.

- ***Practice tolerating discomfort***

Just because you are mentally tough doesn't mean that you don't feel emotions. You should be highly aware of your feelings so that you can choose how to best respond. A mentally tough person accepts his emotions and doesn't let his feelings control him. He also knows when he should behave contrary to his emotions. Maybe your anxiety is preventing you from accepting opportunities or trying new things. You should step out of your comfort zone. Dealing with uncomfortable emotions takes patience and practice. It will become easier as your self-confidence grows.

You should practice acting like the person you want to become. Perhaps you want to be more outgoing. You should start socializing more. It may seem uncomfortable at first, but it's needed for greater gain. Bearing with that discomfort will help make your dreams come true.

How to Develop Mental Toughness at Work

Problems at work can seem so overwhelming that quitting may seem easier than carrying on. However, what separates those who quit and those who persevere is how mentally tough the latter is. There are circumstances when you have no choice but to stop. The most important thing to keep in mind is that you have to develop mental toughness no matter what you are doing or where you are. Here are some tips on how to do it.

- ***Determine what you are working for***

Perhaps you don't know what you are working for. It is time to determine what it really is. Find your goal or purpose. Your goal could be buying a new house or career progression. Maybe you are fine with your job right now because you're saving money for a vacation in your dream country. When you have a goal, you can decide whether you should give up on something. Otherwise, it's not taking you anywhere, or you no longer want to deal with job-related problems. Even if you ultimately decide to quit, at least you know that you made the right decision.

- ***Uphold your standards***

When you are not satisfied with how your career is going, or you are facing problems at work, you might lose interest in your work. You will develop and practice mental toughness by defining and upholding your standards even when you are facing a tough situation. When things don't go as planned, your ability to maintain high standards will help you get through it.

Having a moral compass is also important. What is your viewpoint? Your beliefs define who you are. You will also know the path and direction you should take. It is easy to get confused and lost when you want things to end. Don't be someone who can be influenced easily. You can't really control everything. That's a fact you need to accept. You will have to give up some control so that you can control what is important. This way, you can avoid pointless conflicts.

You have to be prepared for change, as well. Perhaps you are already mentally strong and have defined goals and a strong moral compass. This doesn't mean that you shouldn't let yourself change and grow. True mental resilience is about fighting the need to maintain a behavior pattern or belief system that you or your environment has outgrown.

- ***Internally yourself validate***

Getting pay hikes and hearing praises are gratifying. However, you should validate your achievements internally. This way, it will be easier for you to deal with a rude boss and his habits.

You should also learn to separate your feelings from your problems. It is not easy, but it is the right thing to do. You have to learn how to stay emotionally stable even when problems at work surround you. The best way to do this is to try regularly. Sometimes, you will be required to work harder than usual.

Being emotionally intelligent at work is essential. However, it's also important that you don't allow your emotions to get in the way of your practical decisions and objectives. If your feelings towards situations or people do not influence your mind, your emotional intelligence will be higher.

Conclusion

A mentally tough person can manage his thoughts, behave optimistically, and control his emotions despite the circumstances. You have to be brave enough to create your definition of success and live according to your principles. Always remember that you can improve yourself. Count your blessings, and you will be more motivated to work on your goals.